THE ENERGETIC INVESTOR

THE
ENERGETIC INVESTOR

NURTURING MIND, BODY & INVESTMENT
MASTERY FOR LASTING PROSPERITY

KEVIN BAMBROUGH

LIONCREST
PUBLISHING

THE ENERGETIC INVESTOR
Nurturing Mind, Body & Investment Mastery for Lasting Prosperity

FIRST EDITION

ISBN   978-1-5445-4844-9   *Hardcover*
      978-1-5445-4843-2   *Paperback*
      978-1-5445-4842-5   *Ebook*

.

CONTENTS

AUTHOR'S PREFACE

THERE WAS A TIME IN MY LIFE WHEN I THOUGHT I HAD IT ALL figured out. Ranked number one globally on a five-year basis managing a resource private equity fund, I had founded and grown several of the Sprott group of companies and had risen to be president of Canada's largest and top-ranked alternative asset manager. I was at the top of my game—turning numbers into success stories and crafting financial strategies that defied the odds. Yet, despite the accolades and achievements, I found myself winning my way into burnout and depression while struggling to manage workplace stress and frustrations. The lifestyle I had built wasn't making me happier; it was killing me.

At just forty-three years old, I decided to walk away from it all and then applied the same research and analytical skills that helped me uncover "ten-bagger stocks" to my own life. I asked myself: Could I make strategic investments in my lifestyle that would yield massive returns—not just in life span but in health span? That question sparked an investigation, and this book, *The Energetic Investor*, is the result. It's a deep dive into understanding the true power of energy management and how it can be leveraged for a healthier, more successful life.

The premise is simple: If you want to maximize your health, wealth, and mental abilities, you need to invest in the underlying biological energy systems that power your cells—because ultimately, they power you. This book is about understanding your biology so you can optimize your energy and direct it toward achieving your goals.

The book is divided into three sections:

- **Discover**—Most of us go through life without ever reading the "user manual" to our own biology. In this first section, we explore what makes you, you at a cellular level.
- **Diagnose**—We all have "energy leakages"—habits, beliefs, past trauma, and dependencies that drain energy we should be investing to maximize our performance. Here, we'll help you identify and eliminate those taxing drains.
- **Deploy**—Finally, we explore biologically sound practices that rewire, reframe, and refocus your efforts—so that at a cellular level, you can give your all to the goals you set.

This book isn't just about financial success. It's about the interconnectedness of mind, body, and wealth. I've learned—sometimes the hard way—that focusing on one while ignoring the others leads to imbalance. It's like building a skyscraper on a shaky foundation; eventually, it all comes crashing down. True success lies in harmonizing these elements, creating a life where each pillar reinforces and enhances the others.

When you optimize one area, it naturally fuels the others, creating a dynamic synergy that transforms your life. Think of it as your own personal particle accelerator—where each success amplifies and accelerates the next, generating unstoppable momentum.

Now, let's be clear—this isn't a book about motivation. Motivation is fickle and unreliable; it abandons you when you need it most. Instead, this book is grounded in biology. Science now shows that willpower and habit transformation are deeply dependent on brain energy and metabolic health.

This isn't about getting "pumped up" or forcing yourself to be more intense. It's about implementing practices that naturally lead to transformation because they enlist your biology in the process. There's a science-backed method for change—one that aligns with your biology, rather than working against it. It's about making strategic investments in the fundamental energy systems that power your life.

Throughout this book, you'll gain insights from a wide range of disciplines:

- Psychology & Neuroscience—Learn the cognitive tools used by elite special forces to maintain clarity and control under extreme pressure.
- Biology & Physiology—Understand how to unlock your body's full potential, ensuring your physical health supports your mental and financial pursuits.
- Behavioural Science—Discover how to rewire your brain so that positive change becomes automatic, rather than a constant battle of willpower.

Much of what mainstream outlets tell you is only a fragment of a much larger picture. This book will teach you how to train your biology, so you can truly give your all—where every cell in your body is working toward your vision.

What once seemed impossible will suddenly come within reach through the power of habit creation, automation, and stacking. This process simplifies the path to achievement, allowing each small victory to propel you forward. You'll learn how to invite the flow state into your life, enabling you to operate at peak performance. You'll also retrain your brain's reward center so that positive change is reinforced by your biology, rather than resisted by it.

Ultimately, you'll become the CEO of your own body—managing your health and well-being with the same precision and discipline that a great leader brings to a thriving company. This book is about unlocking your full potential, not just financially, but in every area of life.

By the end of this journey, you won't just be living—you'll be thriving. This isn't about chasing external markers of success; it's about building a life where success is measured in energy, health, resilience, and the freedom to pursue your ambitions without limitation.

You already have the raw materials to create the life you want. What you need is the right operating system to bring it altogether. This book will help you install that system—so you can become the superhero of your own story.

Let's begin.

PART ONE

DISCOVER

What Makes You, You?

CHAPTER 1

WHERE TO START?

I STRUGGLED WITH HOW TO START THIS BOOK. HOW MUCH TO share. How honest to be. But what do my insecurities matter? They are unimportant. Like someone wrote: Your opinion of me is none of my business. And it doesn't change why I wrote this book. I wrote this book to provide you the info that changed me. You can decide where to go from there.

So, let's start with the night my life changed. Having an epiphany. A revelation. Seeing the bottom coming up at you, call it what you will...it was July 19, 2023.

I was sitting on my dock, at my cottage, two and a half bottles of wine deep and had just finished chaining an entire pack of smokes after witnessing a woman I didn't know die. A woman—I believed at the time—I could have and should have saved.

That day didn't start unusually. I was off to the marina. The weather was gorgeous. The boat kicked up a refreshing surf. Nothing out of the ordinary once I moored. The plan was to pick up some materials for a sauna/cold plunge duo I was wanting to build.

While loading the materials from the back of my pickup truck into my boat, I was shocked to hear a woman scream. I snapped my head up and, looking over the front of my truck, saw a small car rolling over the edge of the shore wall. The metal underside of the vehicle scraped over the edge of the steel reinforced pier, while a woman continued screaming, "Oh my God, somebody help"!

With a rush of fear and adrenaline, I kicked off my flip-flops and ran toward the car, pulling off my shirt and throwing my sunglasses to the ground as I ran. The woman at the edge of the dock was still screaming. "Somebody needs to jump in and save her"! she said.

The car had slid off the pier and was upside down in the lake, the front end submerged and the back end bobbing on the water. Steam hissed as the hot underbody hit the cold water and the car immediately began to sink from the weight of the engine. "I think there's a woman inside", gasped the woman at the dock.

I jumped into the lake and swam toward the sunken driver's door. I'd had some lifeguard and scuba training, so I knew to take a few good breaths before diving under the water and to try to keep calm. The murky marina waters had been suddenly disrupted by the weight of the plunging vehicle. Swirling seaweed and mud stirred up from the lake bottom obscuring my view. Straining my vision while feeling around with my hands, I located the door handle only about six feet down. Expecting the pressure outside the car to make opening the door difficult, I placed my feet next to the door seam for leverage and pulled on the handle. It opened slowly, with the pressure equalizing as the car took on water. But the time and effort had me out of breath and unable to see inside the car. I pushed to the surface, took some breaths, and yelled to the people gathering on the dock that I needed a mask.

Back under the water, I reached into the car, fumbling for whatever I could grab. The airbags had inflated, making it difficult to get my arms in. My mind was spinning. Is someone really in here, drowning, and what if I can't get to them? What if they grabbed me and pulled me in, and I drown? Will I find them and not be able to get their seat belt unlatched? But there was no one there. I rose to the surface again, took more breaths, and hollered to anyone who was listening that there was no one in the driver's seat as an image flashed in my mind of the car being left in neutral and rolling in on its own. I was subconsciously considering my risk of getting stuck in the vehicle and dying versus the odds someone was actually in the car that I could save.

I yelled again. "Who saw the car go in? Is there really someone in it"? Someone yelled back that there was a woman inside, so I dove back under the water and swam around to the passenger side, then struggled to open another door. There was no one on that side either. Another guy had jumped in with a hammer, and he asked me if we should break a window. I told him that the doors were unlocked, and I was opening them. I went under again and worked the back door open on the passenger side. Boxes and luggage floated around the back seat. I plunged both arms in, struggling to get my body in past the inflated airbags, feeling around for something soft, like a body. But there was nothing there. Exhausted, I came up for air again. The marina's forklift had pulled up to the pier and marina staff tossed me a chain. Working as quickly as we could, we got the chain to the car's back axle and over a fork, then we all got out of the way in case the chain broke, or the forklift slipped, and the car fell or rolled over in the water.

By this time, the crowd on the pier had grown. The car emerged slowly from the lake, revealing the three doors I had struggled to open and through which it could be seen. Someone yelled, "I see an arm".

I never found out for sure how the car ended up in the lake or the driver, a healthy seventy-nine-year-old woman, had somehow ended up in the back seat on the driver's side—the only place I didn't get to before the forklift showed up. Maybe she wasn't wearing her seat belt and had floated back there. Maybe she was wearing it and had unlatched it and swam back, following the last of the rapidly escaping air. No one knows or will ever know.

The first responders—police, paramedics, firefighters, and coast guard—were all arriving on the scene as her body was pulled from the vehicle, and they all went to work trying to resuscitate the woman. I slowly boated to my cottage as if in a funeral procession. I sat on my dock rather stunned for just over an hour until I got word that despite the medical team being able to restart her heart, the woman had passed. Somewhat stunned and devoid of emotion, I climbed back into my boat and made haste to a store to buy a pack of smokes. On my return, in solitude, I smoked the entire pack of cigarettes and drank two and a half bottles of wine. Come 2 a.m., I was finishing a half-pint of ice cream and stumbling into bed.

We all suffer trauma in our lives. That day at Georgian Bay sure stirred up some past traumas while imprinting some new ones. I was in shock, boating away from the scene, but I didn't know it at the time. I dealt with it the best way I knew how—cigarettes, alcohol, and ice cream.

The following morning, I rose with a headache and a lingering feeling of emptiness and loss. I wandered down to the dock, deep in thought as the previous day's events circled in my mind. Why had I decided to drink and smoke so much? I felt the classic nauseous regret I'd experienced so many times before. I had been on a really good health kick of late and so there was an added sense of disappointment in myself on top of the deep disappointment of not being able to save a woman's life.

As I went about my day puttering on my projects, I was repeatedly triggered. At times, anger, sadness, and deep disappointment rose in me. I'd see a diving mask sitting on a chair and feel a surge of anger inside me as I glared at it, "Sure could have used you yesterday". I'd back my tool cart down the dock ramp and the image of the car sliding off the pier would surface. I decided to take a sauna and swim to shake off the hangover, but surprisingly I felt a strange tingling in my legs as I went to enter the water. It was a strange, very pronounced, and oddly foreign sense of fear to go in the water. I pushed past it, but after diving in, as I opened my eyes, the flight-or-fight chemicals surged in me as I envisioned the car door frame just out of reach in the depths of the dark murky water below me.

It was an epiphany moment for me. My brain and body's wiring had been altered in dramatic fashion as thoughts of underwater swimming had changed from a love's attraction to anxious aversion. It was also perfectly clear to me that I had to explore my drive to drink, smoke, and eat as a form of self-soothing.

WE ARE ALL DIFFERENT IN THE SAME WAY

In this book I am going to talk a bit about what makes us, well, us. Now I am not a doctor, not a scientist, but what I am is a voracious researcher. My research abilities are what made me stand apart, managing more than $10 billion. It was my research abilities which allowed me to retire at forty-three, financially wealthier than I ever dreamed or desired to become. What I researched and discovered since that day helped me become the mentally healthiest and most positively focused person I have ever been. And what I found out applies universally, I think. Sure, we are all different, but the human "machine" is ostensibly the same and can be upgraded similarly.

The first thing that we need to understand is just how much of a team effort *being* is. You are not just "you". You are a collection of biomasses, cellular memories, absorbed trauma (not just yours but your ancestors as well) that are governed by your consciousness, but certainly not defined by it. "You" as you perceive it is only a small part of You (being). It's a lot of yous, I know, but it is important for you to understand that You (consciousness) and You (in its entirety) are not interchangeable. You (consciousness) runs the show for sure but isn't totally in charge. It really is like a CEO that runs the business of keeping *you* you, but it is heavily influenced by your relations to your various parts and the health of the environment you live in (both externally and internally). It's not just about your autonomic systems, but also your emotions, perceptions, and your clarity of purpose. The more you can understand your various parts, enlist them to work for you, and run yourself efficiently, you will be happier, wealthier, and more physically durable.

WHY MOTIVATION ISN'T ENOUGH

What fast food is to nutrition, motivation is to change. Yes, both do their job (kinda) but it most probably will be temporary and unreliable in creating lasting satisfaction. B. J. Fogg mirrored this sentiment in his book *Tiny Habits*, where he labels motivation as fickle and unreliable. Luckily, Fogg argues that motivation and ability compensate for each other. When something is easy to do (high ability), you need less motivation to do it. So successful behaviour design usually relies on increasing ability.

Focusing on incremental changes in habits which will accumulate into higher and higher ability that leads to improvement is a much more efficient use of our energies than keeping on the cycle of motivation and lack of motivation, which leads to you going nowhere.

As the saying goes, if you want to move a mountain start by carrying a stone. That is what we are going to do here. Focus on small changes that accumulate into massive ones.

Becoming the superhero of your own story. I am sure you are familiar with sayings like, "life isn't a dress rehearsal" or some version of "you got one shot". Again—and we will get into it as the book progresses—this idea of conscious change that you just need to be more intense, is a sure way to fail. And to be honest a lot of industry is betting on it. There are countless dollars spent on temporary fixes that are attractive in the short run but don't last. You can see this in diet, well-being, motivational coaches, tinctures, and potions.

Want to become the superhero of your own story? Then don't worry on the "after photo"; focus on the small moves which will be permanent. In the gym, trainers often say we overestimate what we can do in ninety days, but underestimate what we can do in a year. You need to think of change as a series of stackable habits. Habits should be small, but permanent.

CHAPTER 2

WHO IS IN CHARGE HERE?

WE NEED TO UNDERSTAND WHO IS ALL WORKING THERE AND what is the power balance in our body. How in charge are you really?

Your GUT: In any human body there are around 30–40 trillion human cells, but our microbiome is made up of an estimated 39 trillion microbial cells including bacteria, viruses, and fungi that live on and in us.

Even though these organisms make up only about 1–3 per cent of our body mass, this belies their power.

According to Professor Tim Spector—who runs the TwinsUK research unit at King's College—our microbes are more influential in shaping who we are and how we feel than our genes.[1]

We have around 20,000–25,000 genes in each of our cells, but the human microbiome potentially holds 500 times more.

Moreover, the ability of microbes to evolve quickly, swap genes,

---

1   Gaby Roslin, "Secrets of the Microbiome: In Conversation with Tim Spector," *The Bath Magazine*, January 2, 2025, https://thebathmagazine.co.uk/secrets-of-the-microbiome-in-conversation-with-tim-spector/.

multiply, and adapt to changing circumstances give them/you remarkable abilities that we're only now beginning to fathom.

Not to mention mood regulation. The gut has a direct link to your brain. And the conversation goes 90 per cent one way from the gut to the brain. What is really interesting is that researchers are realizing how much impact on our mood a different gut biome has. Different gut biomes literally try out which emotions to trigger in you to modify your behaviour. Some gut biomes like the food you eat when you are anxious. So, guess what? That biome will message your brain to panic trying to get you to eat the foods it wants. Feelings of depression, stress, nervousness, can all be traced back to particular biome activity.

Epigenetics: It is a change in gene expression, without the alteration of genetic code. One of the most comprehensive studies on epigenetics was the Dutch Starvation Study. It proved that unborn children, in fact children that weren't even conceived yet, had their gene expression altered even though it was their parents, grandparents, or great-great-grandparents who suffered the trauma of starvation. You are carrying around the effects of trauma not only you have suffered but the trauma your parents or grandparents have suffered. Your physical connection to your ancestors via their epigenetic switches is very real and has real impact on who you are.

Mitochondria: Around 2.8 billion years ago a tiny marine-like bacteria, now known as mitochondria, began to make its home inside other single-celled organisms. Every cell in every past and present member of our plant and animal kingdoms has contained mitochondria. Mitochondria are not independent creatures but rather essential organelles within human cells. Their evolutionary past as free-living bacteria explains their unique features, but they are now inseparable from the cells they inhabit. Without mitochondria, energy-intensive tissues like the brain, heart, and muscles couldn't function. Studying mitochondria and their bacterial relatives has provided insights into aging, disease, and cellular biology, demonstrating the enduring relevance of this ancient symbiosis. Their existence is a testament to the deep interconnectedness of life on Earth.

I am not positive why you picked up this book, but I bet making money had something to do with it. So, what is with this biology talk? Trauma talk? Epiphanies? What relevance does it have? Let me explain:

Successful investment requires clarity. Clarity comes from synthesizing as much information as possible in the purest form. Purity comes from being unfiltered. The issue is that the way that we perceive the world is filtered through how we register things and what we value. Our emotions, our history, our bloodline, our gut health, and our relationship with our mitochondria can distort how we perceive versus what actually is.

The process through which you will evaluate your own trauma, bias, beliefs, and assumptions will aid you in analyzing the markets. Same tool, different task. The foundation of it all is to understand our biology as it applies to the individual and how it applies to us as a group.

ASSIGN OR BE ASSIGNED

In our economic system, everything is up for sale. That is the reality of capitalism. And I am not complaining or celebrating this. Just laying it out here. And one of the things that we resist accepting is that our behaviour—collective and individual—offers a tremendous business opportunity to those who understand our biological being. Meaning, there is a business and profit incentive in figuring out how to market goods based on making you feel good or feel bad biologically speaking. There is an industry devoted to learning different ways to hijack your reward center including dopamine, the neurotransmitter which plays a role in how we feel pleasure and rewards. We use shame and fear in programming social media algorithms. Big tobacco when it took over big food focused on biology when designing the new wave of ultra-processed, highly addictive foods.

In fact, wellness, pharmaceuticals, fast food, diet, fitness, supplements, snacks, candy, coffee, booze, drugs, politics, medicine, fashion, in fact almost all areas of commerce can benefit from understanding your triggers and marketing to them. And if I can make you feel good, then feel bad, then good again turning you into a repeat customer, even better. And as data collection becomes more and more specific and ubiquitous, the ability to hijack your reward center response is becoming very, very good.

And we all help: We celebrate/commiserate with booze, sugar, fat, drugs. We are more and more dependent on the dopamine hits our phone provides. We pay to move at gyms. Choose drugs instead of lifestyle change. And it is such an ingrained behaviour from childhood that we continue "rewarding/soothing" ourselves even though we know that it will shorten our lives. And it is across racial, gender, and economic demographics. We all are used to outsourcing our dopamine hits from a very young age.

I AM NO DIFFERENT

Booze, sugar, fatty fried foods, recreational drugs. You know, the four horsemen of celebration. I indulged often. And as I got more and more successful at the game, the game rewarded me with more and better opportunities to poison myself. And I joyfully joined the cycle of feeling good, feeling bad, and buying accordingly. Expensive dinners and crafted booze were countered by spa treatments and vitamin boosts.

So, before we get into the weeds on growing "wealth", we have to understand the interconnectivity of mind, body, and finance as well as those who use the information to hijack our systems for profit. Because the three pillars of mind, body, and finance can be used to spiral us downward or spiral us upward.

A *co-morbidity spiral* is a term used to describe the worsening cycle that occurs when multiple health conditions interact in a way that exacerbates each other, often leading to a rapid decline in overall health. In the context of the three pillars of mind, body, and finance, this describes a detrimental cycle where neglecting or mismanaging one aspect of well-being leads to a cascading deterioration in other areas, worsening overall health and quality of life.

For example, poor physical health, such as living with chronic conditions like obesity or hypertension, can lead to increased stress and anxiety, diminishing mental well-being. This mental strain may then result in poor decision-making in other areas of life, including finances, leading to financial instability or the inability to afford necessary healthcare or wellness activities.

In turn, financial stress can exacerbate mental health issues, leading to a sense of helplessness or overwhelming anxiety, which further hinders the ability to engage in healthy habits or seek appropriate medical care. As this spiral continues, physical health often declines further, with untreated conditions worsening and new ones emerging, while mental health and financial stability continue to suffer. In this way, the neglect of any one pillar—mind, body, or finance—can trigger a co-morbidity spiral, where the impact spreads across all areas, making it harder to regain balance and improve overall well-being.

A *co-vitality spiral* embodies a dynamic and positive cycle where the three pillars of mind, body, and finance interact to enhance overall vitality. This concept highlights the interconnectedness of mental clarity, physical health, and financial well-being, creating a self-reinforcing loop of improvement. By engaging in healthy habits such as mindfulness practices, regular exercise, and sound financial management, individuals can foster a co-vitality spiral that propels them toward greater well-being.

For instance, focusing on the body by adopting regular exercise and a balanced diet not only improves physical health, such as reducing blood pressure or increasing energy levels, but it also boosts mental well-being by reducing stress and anxiety. This improved mental state can, in turn, help a person make better financial decisions. In turn improved financial stability—such as better management of debts or achieving savings goals—can reduce financial stress, leading to improved mental health and more time and resources for self-care practices that support physical health.

This combination of better physical health, mental clarity, and financial security reinforces each other, creating a cycle of continuous improvement. For example, someone who becomes financially stable may be able to access better healthcare or engage in wellness activities that further improve their physical health, while feeling financially secure may reduce anxiety, leading to a clearer, more focused mind. By enlisting all three pillars—mind, body, and finance—individuals can create a co-vitality spiral that supports sustainable and holistic well-being. It's all about maximizing the energy system which powers all aspects of life.

At the atomic level, energy determines everything. When atoms are energetically depleted, their electrons fall to lower energy states, orbits shrink, and their ability to form stable bonds with other atoms dramatically decreases. Just like a tired person withdrawing from social interaction, low-energy atoms literally can't "reach out" and connect effectively with others. This isn't just poetic metaphor—it's fundamental physics playing out in our daily lives.

This atomic behaviour scales up to affect molecular bonds and cellular communication. When molecules lack energy, they become less stable and less capable of maintaining proper structure and function. Our cells, which rely on these molecular interactions, begin to falter in their communication networks. Think of it like a city-wide power shortage: When energy drops, the lights dim, communication systems fail, and the whole city struggles to function cohesively. In our bodies, this manifests as reduced cellular signaling, compromised mitochondrial function, and diminished information processing—our biological network starts to break down.

The final expression of this energy cascade appears in human behaviour. Just as low-energy atoms can't form strong bonds, and depleted cells can't communicate effectively, humans with low energy struggle to maintain meaningful connections and process complex information. We make snap decisions because our cellular network lacks the energy for deeper analysis. We withdraw from social interactions because, at a fundamental level, our biological system lacks the energy required for meaningful engagement. The same principle that prevents atoms from bonding prevents us from bonding with others—it's all about energy availability and the capacity to reach beyond our immediate state to form meaningful connections.

Small side note. I am not trying to make you all sober, that is not my endgame. What I do want to achieve is making you sober to the likely future you will experience based on the choices you are currently making consciously and subconsciously. I want to give you the tools to plot your own course as well as the skills to navigate it. My endgame is to make you an independent thinker who has as few distortions on information as possible and can make up their own mind. Hey, we are all going to die, I just want you to have an informed choice on your demise. As Bukowski said, find what you love and let it kill you.

I am, right now, in love with a youthful energy level. And so, I want to extend my functional existence. That takes financial resources and a game plan. In order to have clarity in formulating the best plan and obtaining an appropriate amount of resources, I must gather as much information about the external and internal factors that drive me.

HOW DID WE GET HERE?

To be clear, my love of the "four horsemen" (booze, sugar, fatty fried foods, recreational drugs) didn't start at Sprott Asset Management. (More on Sprott later.) I always indulged. When I was young, I was looking for a good time and felt I was invincible. But there was a darker edge to my indulgences. A darker edge that comes from my father.

My father was an alcoholic. And he died of liver failure at fifty. I am fifty-four as I write this.

My father was high functioning for sure. Was an amazing engineer and business builder. A sharp businessman who worked long hours to provide. Like so many of us, he capped off a busy day at the office with a stiff drink and unhealthy food. Eventually that post-work cocktail spiraled into almost nonstop drinking. Couple that with the TV dinners and couch sitting after a whole day of sitting at the office and, well, it adds up. My father personified the co-morbidity spiral.

Decades later, I am still dealing with his death. I absorbed so much sadness and anger as I grew up, oblivious to the reasons why. By the time he was near the end, I was a depressed university dropout who found comfort sleeping under the pool table in our basement rec room. I was lost and found solace hiding in the quiet darkness.

And when he finally passed, I did what many men do when depressed; I isolated myself. At that time, my depression ran deep. I felt like I was doomed to follow in my father's footsteps. That the world wasn't worth living in, at least not sober. That all the things on the news, the problems of the world, justified and in fact required a stiff drink to help escape from. I imagined that being sober was too emotionally painful for people like me and my father. I felt as though it was somewhat inevitable that I needed to indulge in things that hurt me in order to make life worth living. Funny enough, it took time, but I believe I got so into research as a similar way of escaping. I could distract any internal auditing if I just submerged myself into something else. Anything else. I read voraciously.

The more I read, the more you could see the results of what Noam Chomsky calls a *confluence of interests*. Our society is run by powerful institutions that have a similar formation, similar outlook and goals. To that end there is no need for some supra-governmental council that runs the world. Their similarities and the similar way they pursue interests have resulted in a power structure that obviously wants to protect itself (we all want our survival at the very core of our being) and acts in a similar way.

This societal drive in the same direction grooves mental patterns in us without us really being aware. But if we have done the same things consistently through our lives it becomes a rail track that is hard to jump off of. So, by design, for the betterment of institutions and power structure perseverance, the system pushes us to conform to a particular form of thinking and being. Individual behavioural modification to ensure institutional survival. *The Matrix*, right?

But because it is a confluence and not a structured alliance, there are opportunities by examining human herd mentality and institutional inefficiencies/errors and betting the other way. This realization was the beginning of my contrarian investment style.

CHAPTER 3

THINKING AND INVESTING

THE FOUNDATION OF INVESTING STARTS WITH LEARNING financial history and how to assess risk to reward. We need to counter our evolutionary instincts, and concepts like safety in numbers. Just because everybody else seems to be buying something does not mean that you should be buying it too. Keeping up with the Joneses, so to speak, along with the fear of missing out (FOMO), can be a powerful influence on the human psyche.

However, I don't completely ignore these trends. When everyone's flocking to one thing, they are leaving something else behind. I learned this early on, and trained myself to be a contrarian investor, which somewhat matched my family's instinct to be very suspicious of things that seem too good to be true.

When a sector starts getting lots of attention, I've always cautiously dug in and done my own research to gauge its investment worthiness. Does it check all the boxes? Does it have excellent risk to reward characteristics? Typically, it doesn't. My focus always goes to where most aren't looking; what sectors have been neglected and starved for investment? That is where I've always uncovered deep value and excellent risk-reward opportunities. When I find investments that could make huge gains, I get goose bumps. I've become wired to feel energized when I start uncovering great opportunities. This is the path to follow. It's akin to our ancient hunting instincts to take the path less taken in the hopes of finding untapped plentiful new hunting grounds.

Alone in a forest of possibilities both prey and predators lurk. You hear something and approach it with heightened interest and the endorphins start flowing. It's electrifying when we see the opportunity to bag a big win. We need to remain calm and use all our hunting skills to succeed in capturing it.

I'm typically not looking at the current trending investments, because by the time the average person hears about those, it's often too late to get in and generate huge outperformance. There's an old saying that you should buy what's being written about on the back pages of the newspaper, before it becomes the front-page headline. Find the right stories early and there's a huge profit to be made as they evolve to become news leading.

Joining a crowd feels good though. It's like a shot of endorphins. Excited crowds bubble over with energy—who wouldn't want to be part of a happy optimistic energetic group? If we develop a good understanding of how the markets work, we begin to temper those feelings and eventually we can be triggered to feel aversion from crowded investments.

For newbie investors, the more popular the more attractive: "Wow, all these people believe in this investment, I want to believe in it too"! They want to join a team where everyone is destined to get rich. I mean, if it's true, the results would be phenomenal and life-changing. The prospect is intoxicating.

When we've never suffered big losses, we have our guard down and are more susceptible. Once we've made some bad investments or once we've been scammed, we become cautious. People who have suffered painful losses become skeptical of investing. Really large painful losses lead them to not even want to look at the stock market.

They become wired to believe that every big story is going to turn into a catastrophe, or they just get consumed with negative self-talk and narrate a future with them as an incapable loser.

Many times, I've even heard stories of how someone's grandfather lost the family fortune and how the family and children swore off investing forever. I now realize that these sorts of extreme losses and their emotional trauma get wired into people epigenetically and aversion to managing finances is passed on to their descendants.

The cycle of aversion and avoidance of financial matters can be repaired with strategies like the lifestyle changes I am writing about in this book. It's key to identify financial trauma that might exist in you early and heal it before it disrupts learning and interferes with opportunities to build new positive experiences. An extremely conservative approach that builds on positive returns should be sought out in an effort to build or restore confidence.

We learn to avoid the herd mentality when we realize that bubbles form when the masses flock to the same investment. It's like a hot housing market, when interest rates drop and everyone wants to buy a house, or a second house. Supply can't meet demand and prices run skyward reinforcing the prevailing wisdom that the investment is a no-brainer.

The same thing happens in the stock market. If enough people come to believe that a stock or sector is going to take off, even if fundamentals don't justify it, prices still rise as they buy in with increasing numbers and the positive performance attracts more belief in the investment theme, which then attracts additional speculators to join, and so on. Part of this results from groupthink and that wanting to be part of the crowd.

Another factor is each investor knowing that if everything falls apart, they won't look too stupid, because they were just doing what everyone else was doing. And so, the feeding frenzy begins. People who jump in late may still see a little profit at first, but it's only a matter of time before the market slides and those investors start seeing losses. Some may sell early and take a small loss and move on. But most often, newbie or unseasoned investors just hang onto these investments to the point where they've lost so much that they don't even want to look at them. They hope that someday those stocks will bounce back, and they'll at least get their money back, but this is extremely unlikely; bad investments typically just get worse.

The part of us that made the investment is also often shielded by one or more of our protective parts. We find ways of distracting ourselves from even looking at our portfolios. We prefer to be in a state of denial, not admitting to the loss. "It's a long-term investment, not a bad trade". It's too hard to admit that we made a huge mistake and that the money we worked so hard for is gone forever. Major losses can be devastating and can turn a person off trading or investing forever.

When stock bubbles start popping and breaking down, things go from bad to worse quickly. Over the past many decades, each time major stock market bubbles collapsed, central bankers slashed interest rates and even bailed out some companies or sectors. This nearly never changes the fortunes for the bubble sectors—they are doomed to decline—and instead there's sector rotation.

In my youth, I witnessed firsthand how most of my generation were badly burned by the tech and dot-com market meltdown that started in the year 2000. During that time, people who had been saving and investing for the past decade saw their savings—and sometimes, their retirement accounts—become decimated over the course of just a year or two. Nearly everything listed on the high-flying Nasdaq dropped by 90 per cent or more. This is one reason so many people turned to very broad S&P 500 index funds and mutual funds, and switched from trying to stock pick to just paying fund advisors to invest for them. The thinking was, "I'm no good at investing, I'm never going to let this happen again. I need a professional to make financial decisions for me".

Today there are so many young people that have a hugely inflated sense of their investment skills. Strongly upward-trending markets make every buy-the-dip investor feel like they have the magic touch. Then along comes a serious bear market that destroys nearly everyone's confidence. Many investors gave up on self-directed investing, as winning was replaced with routine losses. It wasn't just a loss of interest; they slowly became wired with an aversion to managing their portfolios. The result was a massive switch to "safe index funds" and "large blue chip low fee mutual funds" and has simply resulted in another historic bubble. It's as if everyone has been thoroughly convinced that dip buying low fee index funds is the no-brainer thing to do. Valuations investing rules of the past have been written off because "they don't work anymore". When nearly nothing in the stock market is cheap and nearly everything is overvalued that's exactly what should be expected. Traditional investment metrics are saying "stay out of this market", but brokers and fund managers always find ways of justifying that clients should pour more money in for "the long term". Well, of course the financial industry always sells this message, because they want trading commissions, banking fees, management fees, and incentive fees. Plainly put, they want your money.

Back at the peak of the bubble of 2000, or just prior to the financial crisis of 2008, I'd try to help warn some relatives or family friends that were retired/nearly retired about the huge downturn I saw on the horizon, providing detailed insights and convincing logic. I advised them to consider getting out of the market for a while or at least raise some significant cash in their portfolio. Their responses were, "If that happens, we are all doomed to lose", "I'm going to stick with my investments and ride it out", and "The government will save us from that scenario". It was also often explained to me that the biggest fear they had was underperforming compared to their friends and not being able to afford a retirement similar to their buddies'. They didn't desire outperformance and instead focused on the comfort of doing exactly what their peer group was doing. It dawned on me that most people's aversion to individual underperformance versus their peers' is a far greater motivator than outperformance or even capital preservation.

It became apparent to me the fear of being the only one ruining their retirement was a blinding force that prevented rational logic-based investment decision-making. The emotional fear of loss increasingly grows more powerful as we age, while taking risks to become wealthier diminishes.

Here's a good analogy to drive home a point about crowd behaviour. A herd of deer graze in the long grass and just one of them thinks it sees a wolf approaching. It decides to bolt and plans to run just fifty feet in the other direction and then stops to look back. It then realizes it didn't see a wolf but just another small deer approaching. Still, this knowledge comes too late as it had spooked the entire herd and it's now unable to stop them as they run away. This is exactly what happens when what might start as a sound investment trend becomes taken over by the madness of a crowd. No one is doing the risk-reward assessment any longer and everyone else thinks someone else smart must know what's going on. Rising stock prices and excited commentary continue to attract more to the trend regardless of the deteriorating fundamentals.

MY LIFE AS A DAY TRADER

After my father's death I was adrift. I knew I wasn't going back to university, but I couldn't hide under the pool table indefinitely. My love of computers, researching, and willingness to self-teach saw me climb from my suburban basement to the top of the banking sector as a computer consultant. Finally, in the late 1990s, I found myself in a day-trading office on the edge of the financial district in downtown Toronto. There were hundreds of people from all walks of life on the second floor where most of the trading happened. Picture row after row of computer desks, with multi-monitors and sleek office chairs. For the first time, individuals like me could jump on a computer that enabled direct access trading on the stock exchange. We struggled to memorize and utilize many keyboard shortcuts necessary to execute trades with the touch of a button, buying and selling stocks through various electronic communication networks.

The owners of the office made their profit by charging us trading commissions and offered us lower trading costs as our trading volume increased. This required us to generate minimum monthly commission totals to at least cover the cost of our office space and computer equipment. Either that or we had to make up the difference by paying the expenses out of pocket. Generating commissions to cover our office costs was therefore a big incentive to do a lot of trading. If we could get in and out of stocks and simply cover the commission cost, it would help pay our bills. In my earliest days there I often played around just trying to catch little intraday-momentum-driven moves in the market to make small dollars and pay for my spot on the trading floor. I got quick on the keyboard and often made one hundred to two hundred trades a day while generating some decent but small profits.

When starting out, my main goal was to just survive in this game so I could learn. Eventually, I was able to slow down my trading volume and look more for smart short- and long-term trading opportunities rather than trying to grab dimes and quarters trading minute to minute. I focused on trying to increase both the frequency of making successful trades as well as making more money when I was right than I lost when I was wrong. Trying to play market maker and just make spreads or gamble on intraday stock patterns is exhausting and not so mentally stimulating. Even the most skilled traders typically got bored with that style, burned out in a few months or at most a couple years. But it was what a lot of traders set out to do because for a time it was very profitable for those that developed the skill. At the time there was so much dumb buying and selling stocks via slow clumsy trading software, while making decisions based on delayed news feeds, that it was easy to reliably predict even short-term stock moves and capitalize on them.

To open an account and be given a desk, would-be traders needed to have at least $25,000 USD in their account. Most people seemed to be coming with at least $50,000 to $100,000 and a lot of hopes and dreams. Even with this limited capital, the access to margin, where you were borrowing money backed by the brokerage, enabled you to trade much larger sums intraday. Leverage of ten to one was available for those who dared. So, with just $50,000 in your account, you could buy up to $500,000 worth of stock on an intraday basis. Some stocks might swing 5 to 10 per cent intraday, so if you could capture that move with a $500,000 trade, you could make or lose $25,000 in one day, or half of your capital on just a 5 per cent swing. There was a huge potential for gains and losses. High-stakes excitement that could send you home feeling like a huge winner or send you packing, broken in spirit and broke financially, never to return.

Some people did manage to do very well. They were like celebrities in that office, and mostly they all sat together in the front corner of the trading floor. They didn't share a lot about what they were doing, especially with the newbies who were generally rather clueless. They figured most of us would screw up, go broke, and be gone in a few months and that's exactly what continued to happen. So, as people left and seats opened up, those that survived would try to work their way forward toward the group of successful traders with the hope of learning from them. It took probably six months, but I survived my initiation to becoming a full-time investor and was able to get a seat in the row right behind them.

The firm gave each of us two monitors for trading, and I splurged on a four-monitor Bloomberg terminal costing $2,000/month—more than twice what I was paying in rent for my apartment. I wanted to give myself the best chance to become a full-time trader and knew if I did, I'd never look back. So, that meant doing all I could to find an edge and seek out repeatably profitable patterns. My desk was the only one in that office out of the hundreds of traders with a Bloomberg. There was a lot of curiosity as to what I was trying to do with it. Still, most everyone felt it wasn't worth it, but a few offered to kick into the cost if I shared the info I was pulling off it. We all knew it was the fastest way to get news, but the key was still going to be reading and comprehending the news fast enough for the extra time to matter. I ordered the full package of newswires and leveraged my IT background, creating news filters to quickly access the types of stories I was looking for from the news feeds.

I experimented with Bloomberg while also watching and learning from the successful guys, always trying to develop my own methods and find my own style. I was slowly able to stop wasting any mental energy trying to generate commissions to fund the monthly cost of my desk space. My account grew and I developed skills and systems that were highly profitable and repeatable. That meant trading less frequently or not at all on some days. It meant exercising patience, holding out the best entries into stocks and holding on to capture the most from stock moves I was able to predict. I looked for opportunities to make larger percentage returns while maximizing my rate of success. I had to manage the risks and the rewards, something I learned about from reading a lot of books on investing strategy. I slowly became well acquainted with the top traders as I earned their respect. One guy, we'll call Bill, started with $25,000 and turned it into about a million and a half, in just the two years prior to me joining the office; he went on to grow it into millions more. This was a very busy, intense, and sometimes intimidating guy. He always seemed like he was in a hurry and under a lot of pressure. He'd sometimes be deep in highly volatile trades with huge, rapidly changing positions and the computer system would crash, leading to red-faced cursing and yelling in total outrage. Unlike most of the guys grouped in the front corner, he often talked loudly about his plans so everyone could hear him. He'd sometimes rant about what he thought was going to happen almost as if he believed his rants would help manifest it. When he went on a rant, everyone quieted down and listened, hoping to gain some edge to make money with. I always marveled at how completely wired he was with his trading style. His trading persona would be on display without him even realizing it. He would be talking about his commute and how it would typically take an hour to get to the office, but he'd managed to cut it down to forty-five to fifty minutes. He figured out that the quickest way was to always stay in the lane that was ending until the last second, then jump onto every off-ramp, only to cut back into traffic at the last possible second. This meant crossing solid lines and sometimes hugging the highway shoulder until a space opened up. That way of driving summed up how Bill did everything, including trading.

That kind of active aggressive trading required fighting on the computer screen all day trying to snatch appearances of mispriced stock. Snagging the best stock entries and exits available. Sometimes the stocks become illiquid, with very few bids or offers, so you must hit opportunities quickly or risk missing them entirely. It's very intense, competing against all the other day traders that might be watching the same stock as you, and competing for the best stock fills.

Often as day traders we would flatten our positions before lunchtime so we could take a break and have lunch out of the office. It was very risky to keep big day trades open over lunch or even go to the bathroom. I can remember sometimes people screaming with anger when some news broke, and they lost $5,000 or $10,000 simply because they were in a highly volatile trade and gambled leaving it open while using the washroom.

Another example of wiring stood out to me one lunch hour when I was walking with a buddy looking for an empty bench to eat our burgers. A bench opened just ahead while a couple approached it in front of us. My friend spontaneously sprinted ahead of them and sat down on the bench to their shock. He looked up at all our faces and then gave the couple the bench, apologizing, "I don't know what got into me". We laughed as we walked away realizing exactly what it was. Our trading styles were affecting us. It was making us ruthlessly aggressive when it came to acquiring and disposing of things. Our brains' wiring was becoming altered, and we knew we had to sometimes check ourselves.

But in the office, it was often dog eat dog, where someone would bet short the same stock that the guy next to him was long. Taking high-stakes opposing bets against people in the same room sometimes led to shouting matches. Especially when one person started loudly cheering on a stock moving in their direction but against others. It got pretty heated sometimes and personal for some.

The people in that room came from all walks of life. There were guys like me, who committed to try to become all-in full-time traders. There were also some doctors, lawyers, and a dentist who'd come in just a couple of days a week. They griped about being unhappy in their jobs and feeling the need to try investing to see if they could make a go of it. There were entrepreneurs, construction company owners, real estate professionals, and so forth. They all had one thing in common: funds to open an account and some history of making significant profits during the strong rally of the late 1990s. Most mistakenly believed that making money in the long term would be as easy as it had been for them in the recent past. They all imagined they could make a career of it and all these people were "wired to take the shot".

I was often amazed by how fast Bill's mood would flip. He'd load up on a stock singing its praises, carrying a big swing position, holding the stock for days, and relishing in the profits as it played out his predicted chart pattern. But he also seemed to actually believe the company was "super-hot, going to the moon". He'd rant that it was going to keep going, saying there's no stopping the rally. Then mysteriously, one morning he'd show up, having read something, or having spotted something he didn't like on a chart, and would announce that the company had peaked. "It's over", he would declare, and it wouldn't just be time to take profits. He'd say it was toast and announce he was going short, betting against the company now. So, there Bill would be, premarket trading and early into the morning session dumping his entire position and shorting the crap out of the same stock he was just cheerleading the previous days, or weeks. That wasn't how I wanted to trade. I would have to come up with my own method, and it wouldn't involve that kind of knee-jerk flip-flopping.

CASE STUDY: PALM PILOT

Back in the early 2000s, there was a large company called 3Com that manufactured the Palm Pilot. Remember the Palm Pilot? Most young people won't but it was a handheld device that many believed had a big future prior to the development of the smartphone. Its business was ultimately destroyed buy another highflyer, Research In Motion, that made the Blackberry, which was then crushed by the larger-screen smartphone trend. Well, Bill executed one of the best combo swing and day trades I had ever seen or even read about. He well understood how things would play out after 3Com announced it would be spinning out their Palm Pilot business. Meaning 3Com would be listing the shares of its subsidiary, Palm Pilot, on Nasdaq in conjunction with a capital raise for Palm Pilot, and then distributing their remaining around 94–95 percent stake in Palm Pilot to 3Com shareholders, thereby divesting 3Com's ownership in Palm entirely. At the time, there was a lot of excitement around the product. Tech analysts on Wall Street touted Palm Pilot as the future leader in mobile devices with huge profits to come, making it a hot IPO to get in on. When companies go public, brokers take them on a road show to large financial investors to raise capital, i.e., buy shares of the initial public offering. The road shows were designed to create maximum investor interest. The IPO price was often set at a level low enough to purposely attract great oversubscribed interest and create momentum. Over time, due to all the tech bubble hype and the pattern of discounting the pricing, IPOs would often yield large instant gains on their first day of trading. So, the new IPO issues began attracting huge interest and traders and investors would put in huge orders for these IPOs, all competing to get stock allocation. Brokers were notorious for giving the best stock allocations to their favourite clients and buddies. The general public who wanted in on the hot IPOs were left out in the cold leaving big instant gains for the guys with the tight relationships. Sometimes these stocks started trading at three, four, even five times the IPO price. So, fund managers or high-net-worth investors that managed to get large allocations of IPO-priced stock could find themselves looking at massive wins on the first day of the stock trading. What made this opportunity interesting was that 3Com was already publicly traded.

Bill's trading theory was that 3Com would rally as the Palm Pilot IPO hype built up. Would-be Palm Pilot investors would sense they weren't going to get a decent allocation of Palm Pilot shares on the IPO, so they would buy 3Com shares as a way to acquire Palm Pilot shares via the share dividend that would occur approximately six months after the IPO. My thinking was that 3Com was already overvalued, and the Palm Pilot was a piece of crap whose popularity wouldn't last. So, I watched as Bill gleefully rode a nice 3Com investment into a significant win as it nearly doubled in the two months leading up to the Palm Pilot IPO date.

Bill came into the office the morning of the IPO excited and ready to execute the big money-making part of his plan. The profitable position he built in 3Com wasn't his main focus. His plan was a work-around for an exchange trading rule that IPO stocks couldn't be shorted as there was no borrowable stock available. His bet was that Palm Pilot would open for trading with a huge gap up on the day of the IPO and then likely give back significant gains as all the dumb money overpaid at the open of trading and the "story" would be somewhat over. The people lucky enough to get big IPO allocations would undoubtedly be scrambling to sell and lock in huge profits during that first day of trading. For 3Com it would be even worse; it would be dead in the water as its other business lines were boring and so the stock was going to drop hard.

Bill had explained his strategy such that nearly everyone in the office knew it and most were going to join him in the trade, myself included, as it seemed to be both a smart psychological trade and one that lined up with my negative long-term bias on both stocks. We waited for the gap up, nervously watching the incredible volatility. As the markets opened many in the office started shorting 3Com. We watched as Palm Pilot stock opened with a massive gap up over the IPO offering price and then started sliding precipitously. Exactly as Bill expected, shareholders of Palm Pilot with free trading stock began dumping shares to lock in their massive profits. Everyone in the office was watching the charts on their screens, regardless of whether they were actually trading it or not. In just the early minutes of trading Bill had successfully exited his 3Com long position and had built a huge, short position, tapping into that huge ten to one margin our broker offered. In a matter of minutes, he had a multimillion-dollar short position, and traders nearby began to watch with amazement as his computer screen oscillated from a large red loss to a huge green profit as the stock swung wildly up and down.

I was sitting right behind Bill and just had my toe in the water with relatively small dollars short, but I cheered my growing profits, along with his. Suddenly, the whole office was roaring as 3Com started dropping like a stone. Some people were screaming because they punched out too early. Others were in a tirade because they had been banging away on their keyboards but were unable to get good fills. Many were just watching, because the stock was too volatile for them, and they were new to the craziness of our day trading office. It was utter chaos, and it was electrifying.

The stock was crashing, then bouncing, then ripping higher, only to crash to a new low again. Finally, the trading volume started to subside as the stock settled into a tighter trading range, down about 21 per cent on the day after having been up in the early morning trading. We all had to struggle to catch our breath, and it was only around 11:00 a.m., and I decided to punch out of the trade with enough profits to make a good month. Bill on the other hand had booked over $1 million in profits just on that intraday trading swing and was clearly enjoying some serious flow state neurochemicals surging through his body. He was beaming as he skipped out of the office on his way to lunch.

My big takeaway was that this kind of contrarian trading style made sense to me. It felt like the direction I wanted to go in. I wanted to learn to predict major moves and then make big scores. I loved how Bill plotted his trades. He could anticipate what the crowd was going to do and then capitalize on his predictions.

The skill was not just being crafty. Bill would often explain he was constantly looking for behavioural patterns in the stock market that he could recognize and successfully trade on with repetition. I wanted to add this technique to my skill set as it would surely improve my entry and exit points into stocks I wanted to bet against or bet for based on my assessment of the long-term fundamentals.

To be clear, by this point I decided that if I was going to be the best trader I could be, I should try to learn all the investing skills I could and then combine them all into one strategy that would work well together. My focus was to develop a complete strategy that I both found interesting and would want to follow for a lifetime. I knew I needed to develop something repeatable that I could become a true expert at. Bruce Lee said, "I fear not the man who has practiced 10,000 kicks once, but I fear the man who has practiced one kick 10,000 times". I wanted to master a technique and was willing to do the training.

CHAPTER 4

THE SPROTT YEARS

MY PATH TO BECOMING AN INVESTOR AND MY EVOLUTION TO professional money management was rather unique. It's probably the number one thing that people have curiously asked me about over the years. I've been asked question after question in this regard. So, it's probably best that I explain how I went from day trading, to hedge fund analyst, then market strategist, private equity manager, to CEO at Sprott as well as president of two separate public companies managing over $10 billion, only to walk away from the industry at forty-three years old.

I had never heard of Eric Sprott, the namesake of the company. The night before our meeting, I perused a few issues of "Markets at a Glance", a biweekly article of Sprott's views. As I skimmed the various PDFs, my interest grew. Mr. Sprott was clearly not an establishment guy, and I passionately agreed with his market views. He wrote about the corruption of the money system, the mal investments it encouraged, and how it was all going to implode leading to a return to gold and silver. That got me excited, so I started googling him. It turned out that despite being somewhat under the radar, especially in the USA financial media I focused on, Eric had a Warren Buffett–like track record. Sprott had compounded capital for a long time at very high rates. I went from not caring much about the meeting straight to caring with nervous anticipation.

Sprott and I hit it off right away. We talked for almost two hours, and I could tell I amused him. He wanted to hear about the various ways I'd figured out to make money short term and long term. I took him through my style of looking for mispriced risk-reward and my hunt for repeatable patterns including some proprietary, rather original techniques and other technical trading strategies I had adapted from books like *Profits in the Stock Market* by H. M. Gartley, a famous technical trader from the early 1900s who successfully traded through the bear market of the 1930s. This is what interested Eric most. He wanted someone to help him with technical analysis and greatly appreciated that like him, I had prepared for a market meltdown and likely decade of choppy investing that could benefit from some technical analysis. He was curious if I could help his investments perform even better. I agreed to join him but professed that I was interested in helping everywhere I could because technical trading wasn't my main skill. He said we'd start with the technical stuff and see where it went from there. He had to just confer with his partners and the next day he called to ask if I could start the following Monday as a technical analyst at Sprott Asset Management, an exciting growing boutique alternative asset management firm with twelve employees and just under $1 billion in assets under management.

More than a regular paycheck, I was excited to see if I could learn even more about the markets and investment strategies from someone who seemed to be in line with my way of thinking. But the opportunity to make huge money had been impressed on me in my first meeting with Eric as he explained the "2 and 20 model". As performance attracted capital, assets under management grew. Then depending on the fund, the firm charged a 1 to 2 per cent management fee and then charged up to 20 per cent of the profits it generated. The goal I quickly imagined was to get over $1 billion under management in that 2 and 20 structure, and then just double it and make a $200 million fee. There were no formulas for fee sharing but Mr. Sprott alluded to his historical generosity while indicating that everyone at the firm was very well paid, wealthy, and happy. Despite having to get a new wardrobe and my hour-long daily commute to the office, I was excited.

I hit the ground running and got off to a great start. Right away he agreed to let me make some trades. But it was a challenge to get time with Eric and his sign-off on my trades. I wasn't a portfolio manager, and so nothing happened without his approval. But if he liked what he saw, he'd act quickly. That surprised me. I'd make a call thinking a couple hundred thousand would be put to work and he'd instruct the trading desk to short $5 million. Some of these stocks didn't have much liquidity, so I quickly learned that I needed to adapt my style to accommodate his size preferences.

Things quickly grew tense as he was managing a huge portfolio, and I could clearly tell he didn't want to waste time looking at small, short-term trades. Even though I was making win after win, I could see that he didn't care about them that much because the numbers were small compared to other stuff he was working on. I was making our portfolios a million here and a million there, thinking that it was phenomenal. I was also imagining the 20 per cent of the profits I was generating going into a bonus pool and a nice end-of-the-year bonus coming to me.

Sprott saw things differently. I was distracting him from the big picture and his hunt for ten-baggers. I could sense growing hostility and frustration with my active trading. He was more interested in his long-term investments. On the short side, he wanted stocks that were going to go down 70 to 90 per cent or terminal shorts that go to $0 and you never even cover.

On the long side, he wanted only stuff that might go up huge. He wanted to invest $10–$50 million in a company and make $100–$500 million. He just wasn't going to be able to spend time managing billions of dollars with me bugging him about little trades that made up just 0.5 per cent of the portfolio. Our relationship really went south in the late summer of 2002, when the market was severely oversold. Sprott believed we could see a total crash like what had happened just four years earlier, in 1998. Despite the oversold nature of the market, he didn't want to cover anything; he was shorting more and playing for the crash. He was very confident and had nerves of steel, adding to shorts as they plunged in a melting market. The hedge fund was performing as planned and was up around 90 to 95 per cent on the year. It was the number one performer in the country, generating massive fees. Suddenly, the oversold market turned and began to rally.

At first Sprott was confident it was just a blip, and the trend down would resume because that's what his fundamentals told him. He pressed me for insights, and I couldn't give him exact percentage odds or anything other than to explain that it was severely oversold and could easily rally back to a major moving average like the fifty-day moving average, which was significantly higher. He argued his fundamental data points about the economy and pushed me to agree that it could also turn and collapse. I admitted that it was possible but that when the market is this oversold it can easily go up a lot as well, maybe another 20 per cent rally. If he played it wrong, he would give up a huge percentage of the profits he'd generated. My lack of decisiveness bothered him. In fact, it seemed to infuriate him in the stress of the moment. I backed off and didn't push like I should have. I was afraid to tell him what I really thought. There was no good in telling him that I wouldn't have been shorting recently like he had. That I was more conservative than he was and would have been content to take profits. I also didn't want to tell him that I wouldn't have been up 95 per cent on the year while managing a billion dollars with a hyperaggressive long-short strategy in that high-volatility market. It was obvious to me that our styles didn't mesh.

For me, if stocks I'm shorting become really oversold in my trading portfolio, my discipline is to take lots of profits off the table. When the entire market is severely oversold, my trading discipline is to focus on buying opportunities in stocks I like. I would dramatically lower my short exposure and increase my long exposure. Eric covered a lot of shorts, giving back some significant profits along the way, we survived the month, and before long, things started trending our way again.

Despite the year finishing up well, he would barely speak to me over the following months, even though I was sitting across from him on the trading desk. It felt like the experiment of having me try to help him with technicals was over. He knew it and I knew it. I couldn't survive in that environment trying to show someone technical trades that they only acted on if they agreed with one part of the trade. I had to find another way to be helpful to him with the funds or go back to just managing my own capital, which seemed like a huge step backward given the firm's assets under management. I continued to focus on major technical calls when names in our portfolio were really overbought or oversold.

I remembered seeking advice from Chris—a broker associate—who had introduced me to Eric. Chris suggested that I needed to be bold to get Eric's attention or I was likely done. I had to be aggressive and not hold back. I came back from the Christmas break determined to make my mark. Upon our return to the office, I laid out some stock picks I had researched over the holiday. Long and short stock picks for January, based both on technical analysis and fundamental value. Plus, the expectation of some of the stocks moving following tax-related year-end movements. Tax loss selling results in stocks going down in December as some investors sell to realize losses and lower their current-year tax bill. Many of these stocks end up having a great January as they were oversold in December and often see the tax-related sellers attempt to buy back their positions. Conversely, stocks that had really great years often rally excessively into overvalued territory into year-end because would-be sellers begin to delay selling, deferring their tax liability an additional year. My January picks were big liquid companies with trade matching fundamentals. As January rolled on, those picks worked out fantastically. My short picks outperformed all our other short positions in the portfolio that month, and my long picks went up significantly as well. Heeding the advice about being bold, at the end of January I pointed out my stock picks' relative performance hoping for some recognition and accolades in the morning meeting. This was my chance to get noticed. I was trying to get Eric to allocate more capital to my trades. I wanted him to see that I could do more for the funds. But I quickly felt my attempt to be bold flopped as Eric merely quipped that recently added positions generally outperform at first. As the meeting ended, he instructed me to follow him in his office. I figured this was it, and I was getting fired.

We went into his office, and he shut the door. We sat across from one another at his desk, and he lit into me. He berated me, raising his voice. He suggested I had a lucky month and that he was focused on many positions and looking for ten-baggers and he didn't care about short-term moves. It seemed the next words out of his mouth were going to be, "So, I'm letting you go" but I wasn't going to give him the chance. I stood up and said, "Look, if you're going to fire me, just fire me. But I'm not going to sit here and have you tear a strip off me and then fire me". He seemed taken aback, and I continued emotionally, "I've been trying my best, I'm trying to help without being annoying. I'm making great calls, and I was told I needed to be bolder and more aggressive". He said something like, "Sit down, I'm not going to fire you". Then we sort of laughed it off.

I think he was glad that I stood up, that I had that kind of spirit. We discussed that when he hired me, he stated that he didn't want another "yes man", and he said the next time I wanted to bring up positioning changes and review them, we should discuss it one-on-one. After that, we started having short but productive one-on-ones in his office and positive open discussions in the very early mornings. I also started to successfully get my macro views heard. There was a major fundamental difference between Sprott's longer-term view and mine. He believed in a deflationary collapse, and I was focused on long-term hyperinflation as an inevitability and at very least periods of very strong inflation following any short-term deflationary breaks in the market.

I believe now and I believed then that the central banks are going to print money and cut rates to zero every time the economy and stock market collapses. They will continually engage in more extreme measures to rally the stock market, bail out the banking sector and key industries, buy up bad debts, and forgive them. It's not going to be about what's fair. It's going to be about survival. Most certainly about the survival of the government bureaucrats in power, survival of the central bankers, survival for the key players in the bank industry.

The banking industry grooms our future central bankers starting in university. It recommended them their positions on the Federal Open Market Committee (FOMC) and the Board of Governors. These people with impressive titles and a lot of initials after their names have been trained their entire lives on the various money-creating mechanisms at their disposal. They are wired to do their jobs, prevent deflation, and save the banking system at all costs. They arrogantly believe that we are all better off because they have unlimited power to print money. Given that, why wouldn't they print and bail when given the chance? It's clearly part of the job description. As if one day some of them will just say, "Screw it, I'm out of here. Let's just let it all fall apart". Instead, it's my belief that we will continually experience greater and greater bubbles rotating from sector to sector as inflation gets progressively worse. Each will require more extreme measures and more printing and bailing. Businesses and the people who "make it" will be determined more and more by their deemed importance in the eyes of the Fed officials and public pressure. The number of people allowed to fail will grow in ever-increasing numbers, as more individuals are hit with dislocating circumstances during each and every down cycle. Individuals will be routinely knocked out of the middle class when they are deemed not too big to fail by the central banking elite. During times of great inflation, government and banking bureaucrats will continue to argue it's transitory and temporary. They will also raise rates in times of severe inflation until they break something. Pop a bubble, crash a market, and throw millions of unsuspecting citizens out of work, out of their homes, and so forth. This will lead to continued societal infighting, blaming, and shaming. The finger-pointing will eventually lead to a swing to greater political interference and more social support from the government. The masses will continue to elect officials that will deficit spend to help their individual causes. Those in the middle class that survive will continually bitch about their taxation and be angry for being forced to support government and its social programs.

Sprott was more in the deflationary camp, believing potential collapses of 90 per cent for all the major indexes, not just the tech-heavy Nasdaq, was possible; 1929 all over again.

We did agree on one thing: gold and silver. But I wanted to convince him that many commodities were going to be important and would have periods of amazing performance as it was clearly overdue. We were at the end of a twenty-year bear market and Eastern-led growth was upon us.

While working with Sprott and company, I focused on everyone's moods and attitudes a lot trying as best I could to read the room and fit in where I could. That's an important skill for anyone in business. I was in a firm where everyone else had advance degrees and industry certification. The boardroom was highly competitive, and it was difficult for anyone to get time with Eric.

Many of the people in the firm were understandably bristly. They all wanted Eric's attention and were rather competitive for it. Partly because of the money at stake but also just because we all endeared ourselves to him, our leader, the one we wanted to help most to better the firm. Eric did foster a hypercompetitive environment that encouraged people to compete against each other in a sort of free-for-all. So, we were all somewhat protective of our spaces. I took the approach of simply trying to be as helpful to everyone as I could, a real team player. There was plenty of money to go around, and if I could help the company do well, I believed that good fortune would shine on all of us.

My focus turned to areas where I excelled, which were the skills I developed earlier at the day trading office. I had become somewhat of an expert on the Bloomberg terminal and could gather and process information quickly. I started monitoring every stock in the company's portfolio and kept an eye on the technical and news for each one.

When a stock was getting overbought or oversold, I'd suggest taking a profit or buying more, respectively. I gave that information and advice to the different people responsible for different stocks, as well as Eric. Then I tracked the news on all of them and helped with updates and technical chart changes. Another change I made was not to discuss my theories on inflation. Eric didn't agree with them—he was still clinging to his deflationary collapse theory and wouldn't listen to anything I had to say on the subject. Bringing it up only made him angry, so I moved on to other topics in conversation. But I would give him articles and blurbs that I dug out of reports of every kind that served as evidence backing my inflationary commodity bull market view. I wasn't the only person leaving papers on his desk—Eric left the office every night with a stack of articles and reports, which he'd read at home, usually waking up between 4:00 and 5:00 a.m. to do his "real work".

Every morning, we had a meeting, where Eric would discuss his views on breaking news and updates on the long-term macro. Bit by bit he started regularly bringing in the information I had highlighted for him and shared it with the group. Often my work formed many of his key talking points and macro themes of the day. Our relationship grew and he started asking me to come into his office for more one-on-ones. When he finally started prioritizing my recommendations, I was elated. He was getting everyone in the office involved, looking for stocks in energy, specialty metals, and other materials. We had missed most of the copper rally but were active in opportunities in minor metals, oil and gas, coal, uranium, potash, and phosphate.

Over the years I became what some would call his right-hand man, helping make decisions and staying on top of the macro. I preferred idea generation and monitoring the macro or "big picture". Eric grew fine with me in this role and often handed off ideas I would generate to other analysts to model in detail. Sitting at the trading desk, Eric and I would make ballpark guesses on what the models would likely show in terms of valuation potential. Confident the answer would be "strong buy" we typically didn't wait for the detailed models to be generated.

Another lesson I learned here was not to care about my title, and I think that's important in any job. In the workplace and in life focus on being as useful as possible. With every promotion I received at Sprott, from technical analyst to research analyst, market strategist, president and CEO of Sprott Resource Corp, becoming founding CEO of our private equity division Sprott Consulting, and eventually president of Sprott Inc., I was being useful and doing all these jobs before I had the title. You can't sit around waiting for an appointment and a new title—you have to show that you can do the job.

People have often asked me about my unlikely rise in the firm despite my lack of credentials. And I like to think it was just the hard work and dedication with desire to help any way I could. If the printer was out of paper, I didn't just slap a package in the tray. I'd get a whole box from storage and replenish the shelves while I was at it. If someone's computer acted up, and I could provide some quick assistance, I'd fix it. I wasn't above crawling under desks to get things up and running. Being a prima donna gets you nowhere.

This is what I told people who asked over the years. I've now changed my mind rather drastically. Yes—I did try to focus on the team and work hard, but that's not why I rose at the firm. The truth is I'm a dopamine addict that got heavily addicted to the endorphin release from the combo of researching, making predictions, being right, and getting paid. Plus, like most high-functioning, high-performing addicts, I am very protective of my ego. When I sense people want me to fail at something I dig down and try to find a way to succeed. The harder I'm pushed the harder I push back. When I was on the bubble of trying to make it at Sprott, more than the money, I needed to prove to others and myself that I deserved to be there. It was plainly obvious that Eric Sprott thought he didn't need me, thought I couldn't help him at first. He had vast knowledge, experience, and amazing work ethic. My only option was to take advantage of all the time I had available that others didn't. I didn't need to go to meetings, I didn't have to take calls, and I had access to all the reports and information the world could offer. I was hungry as hell to learn all I could and I literally got high from it. So, I became all consumed with trying to out read and outlearn everyone at the firm. I supremely focused in what I thought would be emerging trends that could make our clients big money and I dove into these areas with hyper-focus. This was probably my first real experience with sustained flow state or being in the zone. I loved it and found myself wanting to read day and night. Sure, I'd take some breaks to blow off some steam or enjoy fun times with friends and family. But the hours I dedicated to reading were unmatched. It was a very privileged position to be given that level of freedom and access to information in that free-for-all environment. Sink or swim, try to be useful or be fired. That's how we rolled in the early days, and it was a spectacular exciting environment that I flourished in.

I also learned that the financial industry is also somewhat lazy. Most people modeled companies by looking at earnings a year or two out. Eric worked differently, buying up 10 to 20 per cent of a company and staying with it for three years or much more, adding to his position on every capital raise they did. For better or worse. When it worked out, our investments went up as much as ten times, sometimes more, and we'd turn $5 million into $50 million or $10 million into $100 million. When things went poorly, stocks could collapse by 90 per cent, and we'd cash them in for the tax losses.

I've maintained this focus and hunt for the 10x returns but my style has evolved because I'm no longer part of a firm managing billions. As a result, I like to buy early and go big but often take some early profits. Some people will criticize my current method. They often point out how much more I could make if I didn't sell some of my big winners early on. But I'll argue this point all the way to the bank. My system works out very well because so many times these little stocks don't work out as planned. There's also so damn many of them to play. Over time, I end up digging up enough excellent risk-reward opportunities such that I don't mind selling some winners a bit early. I hate losses and love being in no-lose situations repeatedly, and I do this by focusing on only getting in extremely early where I'm nearly always going to catch some of that new-story momentum as the marketplace moves from pessimism to optimism with no change required in the company. This is the art of getting paid by doing the hard work required to see a revaluation coming entirely due to a change in market perception.

LEAVING SPROTT

In 2011, we were still recovering from the 2007 recession, and I wasn't excited about what was going on in the market. We were in a bear market that started in resources like uranium, because of the nuclear accident at Fukushima. After a big rebound, there was oversupply in some commodities, so they were slowing down. China's demands were slowing down too. Going into 2013, the economy was still sluggish, and some sectors were in trouble. Those were turbulent times.

I had agreed to be president of Sprott Inc. while also running a half-billion-dollar private equity fund. I was under a tremendous amount of stress. Then my COO and private equity partner discovered he had Parkinson's disease, and we both began soul-searching about what was really important to us. I was forty-three but fifty seemed to be looming just ahead. Remember, my dad died at fifty. By then, I had enough money, such that I would never have to work again. There were conflicts at work, partly because we had grown so much and there were many more people and strong opinions. In the past decade we had gone from a dozen employees to more than 130, and from managing just under a billion to well over $10 billion. We'd had a great run, and so had I, grossing more money than I'd ever dreamed of, or would ever need.

My private equity fund had just completed a five-year anniversary and reported an IRR of approximately 28 per cent on investments after fees and taxes. The most remarkable part of this return is that the TSX venture was down about 90 per cent over the same time frame. The outperformance was virtually unparalleled as we had returned close to +250 per cent total return versus our bench market down −90 per cent, making our relative return about twenty-five times better.

Sixteen years earlier, I had started investing by funding stock trades with my credit card and I ended up as a key player in many of the top-performing funds in the world, while amassing capital at the biggest hedge fund in Canada. Then, at forty-three, I retired.

People wanted to know why. The short answer? I was burnt out.

The immediate catalyst was I didn't like some of our funds and had a major disagreement with my partners regarding the reopening of a fund that I had fought previously to close. I felt the decision to reopen it was being approved by the investment committee only because the fund needed to raise new funds since it couldn't meet its redemptions. I felt the people responsible for marketing its reopening were obfuscating the truth about the liquidity issues of the fund and were being disingenuous regarding the reasons for the reopening.

The dispute wasn't resolved to my satisfaction and so concluded my days at Sprott. Wish I could say it ended on a more positive note. It took time but around five years after my departure the firm did exit its relationship with the product I was so vehemently against and with today's hindsight they all have come to recognize I was right to take my stand back then.

Looking back, the "dispute", no matter how real it was to me then, really was the final push my body and mind needed to recognize my downward spiral.

I had been focusing so much on the financial part of my life that I totally neglected my body and mind. It was time for a change. I wish I had jumped more into respecting my body and mind sooner, but July 19, 2023, will have to suffice as the beginning of the "new me" and started this journey of discovery.

CHAPTER 5

WHO IS WORKING FOR YOU?

THE PATH FORWARD IS TO ARRANGE YOUR LIFE SO THE THREE pillars of mind, body, and finance act as an accelerator for each other. And the first port of call is to really understand your assets. Let's start with pillar one: the Body.

I briefly touched on the idea that your consciousness is more like the CEO of "you" then being the entirety of "you". For a business, management efficiency is paramount. I think it's also paramount for your health: You must understand and manage "you" like a well-run company. In that "internal audit" there are key departments. The first I want to discuss is the role your gut plays in your success.

Your gut and microbiome ecosystem affect more than you think, including your decision-making. What you eat is not just nourishment in terms of supplies for the body, as it feeds an entire ecosystem of microbes. These microbes can trigger neurochemical imbalances that affect your mood and decision-making around your diet, as well as your ability to deal with adversity and manage stress. Your relationship with these microbes even affects your ability to process information, learn, and remember. Your behaviour is tied to your gut on an unconscious level and in profound ways. The connections are much more powerful than just feeling irritable because you're hungry. We need to think of food as not just energy but instead its effect on our neurochemicals. All foods and drinks have effects on us that are akin to drugs.

THE MICROBIOME OFFICE

What we call the "gut" is short for the gastrointestinal tract, which begins at the esophagus and continues down through the stomach, the large intestine (colon), and the rectum. The entire pathway is populated with microscopic organisms. Every human's individual ecosystem of microbes is unique, and its population is always changing, affected by what we eat and drink. These microbes consist of bacteria, viruses, fungi, and other life-forms. This extremely complex ecosystem is essential to our ability to process food and protect against pathogens, which are other microbes or viruses that can hurt us. The population of microbes in the human gut is estimated to be greater than the total number of cells in the human body—and they are vital to our existence.

GETTING THE BEST PERFORMANCE FROM YOUR MICROBIOME EMPLOYEES

Scientists compare the discovery of the health influences of our microbiome (microbial ecosystem) to finding a new organ, even though it comprises a collection of microorganisms that can be dramatically altered. When you think about it, the gut's microbiome is no more than an enormous collection of independent living organisms surviving in a petri dish. We can control both the makeup and numbers within the population; and when we control the diversity of the population of microbes, it has a drastic effect on our health system. These changes to the microbiome dramatically alter how we break down our food and distribute the nutrients to our bloodstream. We can change the demographics of the microbe population, getting rid of bacteria, viruses, and fungi that harm us and replace them with good microbes, in effect, improving our ability to function. A poorly functioning microbiome is like having a weak organ—a compromised heart or liver. Creating a high-functioning microbiome is like getting an organ upgrade.

Unsurprisingly, you can make this upgrade just by changing what you eat and drink.

Microbes were first observed by Antonie van Leeuwenhoek in the 1670s. It wasn't until the twentieth century that scientists realized their significance in the gut and human health. That knowledge continues today as new technologies and research ramps up. The term *gut-brain axis* is becoming more prevalent in articles and mainstream marketing. Gut-brain axis refers to the directional communication network within the central nervous system. Communication among the plethora of neurons in the gastrointestinal tract is facilitated by microbes, which produce neurotransmitters and other signaling molecules that affect our brain function and behaviour.

Considering all the autonomic functions of the body, these microbes are much more "plugged in" than anyone thought. They can bypass a person's cognitive brain and directly influence and trigger physical (even muscular) reactions and corresponding chains of events, likely in every region of the body. So, right down to the autonomic triggering of our hands, to put food in our mouths when we eat. Adverse microbiome populations and general dysregulation have been linked to serious physiological illnesses and mental health problems like anxiety, depression, autism spectrum disorder (ASD), attention deficit hyperactivity disorder (ADHD), and extreme conditions like schizophrenia. It's possible that these conditions may be improved or even cured with dietary changes that reform a person's microbiome population and change our neurochemistry.

Microbes play a vital role in breaking down food and delivering nutrients. When we are missing certain microbes, we can become deficient in various nutrients. The foods containing these nutrients may simply be passed through our guts without the nutrients entering our bloodstreams.

Our "gut-brain" knows exactly what its microbes like and it wants to satisfy them. It knows what happens when its microbes aren't fed, and we then feel irritable, low on energy, sad, and even depressed. Those microbe-hunger-driven reactions can also swing the other way, causing emotions to run high and even erupt in fits of rage.

When a conversation starts about an event or activity that doesn't involve what our microbes want, our gut neurons immediately give feedback to our cognitive brain, advising us to avoid situations where our microbes won't be happy. This can all happen at an unconscious level and seems like the right thing to do or just an instinctual preference. Conversely, events that make us feel anxious and cause social anxiety produce stress chemicals. Activities like public speaking and other stressful events create microbial-damaging stomach acids, so our gut instinct is to avoid them.

I used to get stressed out before going on TV. In the days leading up to the interview, I was anxious, and my appetite would disappear. I instinctively wanted to say no to TV appearances and usually after doing them, I would tell myself to say no to future invitations because the stress was too much to handle. If you think your most common or powerful fears are all in your head, maybe they're not—they could start in your stomach!

The neurons in your gut cause you to be attracted or repelled and affect your decisions. Do you avoid doing your taxes? Managing your money and investments? Or does the thought make you sick to your stomach? There may be more truth to that statement than you realize.

Once we understand this connection, we can take steps to override our gut reactions and change our instinctive behaviour. When we become mindful of our biological drives, and focus on them, it empowers us to use our cognitive abilities to intercede and course correct. Never lose sight of the fact we have successfully evolved because our top-level cognitive thoughts and decision-making alters our wiring to our benefit.

We will explore this more as we move into meditation and mindfulness but it's worth mentioning here. Missed opportunities and portfolios don't self-correct, and gut-triggered avoidance typically leads to much bigger problems. "The trend may be your friend" is a common investing saying, but the trend is also your enemy when you or your portfolio is down-trending.

There is a lot more going on in your gut microbiome than attraction or repulsion instincts. Our microbes have developed to succeed by influencing us to do their bidding. Some microbes cause us to experience large swings in our neurochemical levels, which are our primary mood- and emotion-influencing drugs. They affect our energy and can stimulate or depress us. When microbes want to be fed, they can trigger a drop in our body's feel-good drugs, serotonin and dopamine, by releasing neurochemical inhibitors that reduce our receptivity to these pleasing chemicals.

When this happens, the gut neurons step in to signal our cognitive brains to head to the restaurant, grocery store, or just wander into the kitchen and browse for exactly what our microbes are craving. Once fed, our microbes thank us by cranking up our feel-good juices (neurochemicals) while turning off the inhibitors.

They can enhance our sensitivity to dopamine and serotonin by releasing neuro inhibitors or thanking us for feeding them by stimulating us. This creates a powerful bond between our thinking and our microbes that is constantly reinforced over time, so we develop a deep, intimate love affair with our comfort foods and drinks. It's easy to slip into a poor diet that feeds an increasingly aggressive microbial population, bringing our gut health further out of balance.

Growing up—just like for most people—celebrations and food went hand in hand. Birthdays and holidays called for lots of foods high in calories and low in nutrients. Weekends meant special treats, like cakes and pies. For me, rich, sweet foods went hand in hand with gatherings of family, friends, and good times. This habit reinforced a psychological drive for comfort foods. The after-school snack became the after-work snack. The car-trip snack became the commute snack.

And so on. It would be easy to blame my adult eating habits on my childhood, but I realize my cravings went much deeper. Deep as the neuron in my gut's programming, where there was a lot going on that drove my behaviours without my knowledge.

I read many an eye-opening study regarding various dominant microbes and their behaviour-influencing techniques. The main chemical levels that can be messed with are serotonin and dopamine, pleasure chemicals, but some target the neurotransmitter gamma-aminobutyric acid (GABA), which can flip us from relaxed mode to being anxious. Others target norepinephrine (noradrenaline), which influences alertness and arousal. There's also acetylcholine, which influences muscle signaling and can affect cognitive function. These can all affect our mood and ability to concentrate and learn.

Consider when you're really hungry and too tired to even think about what you want for dinner. This is when we often give into our first instinct, which sadly, for many people like me, is often something quick, easy, and exactly what the most dominant microbes want. Microbes have also been shown to target and affect muscles too. They can adjust the speed at which food moves through our intestinal tract, as if they are choosing to slow down peristalsis, or speed it up when they don't like what's on the menu. It's sort of amusing to imagine microbes causing diarrhea to get rid of food they don't want, sending the message, "get this out of here, try again".

Our melatonin levels can also be tampered with by microbes, which affects our sleep-wake cycles. Our microbes can wake us up at night and tell us to get them a snack. They can lower our melatonin levels while also firing us up by messing with our ghrelin levels. They can turn our hunger signals on and off.

Some of the more well-known, nastier microbes crave sugar and carbs. Candida, for example, can punish us by generating feelings of depression or anxiety. Or they can give us a short-term energy spike of relief when we feed them. If candida microbes get hungry, they can make us feel weak, upset, anxious, and depressed. They train us to feed them in order for us to feel better. When they get their "fix", they stop inflicting us with pain and anxiety. This is why it's so difficult to give up sugar and carbs.

From Roseburia, we get big serotonin rewards. Firmicutes, often associated with obesity, are said to love fast food and sugary snacks and also spike our dopamine. Then there are various types of lactobacilli, which enjoy fermented sugars and alcohol. They can release GABA to give us temporary stress relief, which is why we sometimes feel like we need a drink to calm our nerves.

Lactobacilli may give us temporary stress relief, but longer term, feeding them alcohol has negative effects. There are over eighty common varieties of lactobacilli in most people, such as lactobacillus reuteri, found in fermented foods. They can hit us with serotonin and affect GABA levels to reward us for giving them food like yogurt, kefir, kombucha, and cheese. (You might think you need an alcoholic drink, but as you get used to a new diet, you might find that you can relieve your anxiety and stress with healthier options that aren't likely to turn you into a couch potato.)

For many people, gut neurons become emotionally dependent on alcohol or certain foods because it's worked for them in the past. But you can completely retrain them. It takes time, and a determined microbial repopulation effort, but you will get to a point where these alternatives make you feel not just as well, but much better. Plus, you'll have the benefit of avoiding the ill side effects of alcohol and unhealthy foods. The best microbes don't punish you by making you feel weak by not feeding them. A healthy, well-diversified population of microbes doesn't drive the bus so aggressively and has much better table manners.

You can keep going down this rabbit hole for days. The variety of microbes is endless. Bifidobacteria, found in bananas, reduces stress with GABA, so eating a banana can make you feel calm. Faecalibacterium prausnitzii gives us butyrate, which comforts us and provides stress relief.

Countless microbes contribute to serotonin, and it's worth noting that 90 to 95 per cent of the body's serotonin comes from the gut, while only 5 to 10 per cent of our supplies are synthesized or made within our brain. This is why comfort foods are so extremely powerful. It's no wonder they're so addictive. Again, the reason I am taking a side trip into biology is that you have to understand what is influencing your ability to synthesize information and make judgments. How is your gut? Maybe it's time for a performance review.

So, you have done a gut check. What other internal checks should you be doing?

MITOCHONDRIA

Mitochondria is so much more than the "powerhouse of the cell". Besides the fascinating history of how a bacteria got together with your cell and worked out a symbiotic relationship, the mitochondria is such an important department you need to take a look at. It would be impossible to function without them.

Sure, these organelles generate adenosine triphosphate (ATP), the primary energy currency of the cell, through a process called oxidative phosphorylation. ATP fuels vital functions such as muscle contraction, cell division, and protein synthesis, making mitochondria central to the body's ability to sustain life.

But beyond energy production, mitochondria are involved in many other critical functions. They regulate cellular metabolism, help maintain calcium homeostasis, and play a pivotal role in apoptosis, or programmed cell death, which is essential for removing damaged or dysfunctional cells. Mitochondria also produce reactive oxygen species (ROS) as by-products of energy production, which, when properly regulated, play a role in cell signaling and immune responses.

Speaking of which it's now becoming clear that mitochondria don't just provide the energy for signaling between cells, they have their own network and dynamic synaptic connection system at the foundation of our cognitive processes.

Mitochondrial health is particularly important because dysfunction in these organelles is linked to a variety of diseases, including neurodegenerative disorders like Parkinson's and Alzheimer's, metabolic conditions like diabetes, and even aging. This highlights their fundamental role not just in cellular function, but in maintaining overall health and preventing disease. In essence, healthy mitochondria are vital for energy production, cellular health, and the organism's ability to adapt and thrive. Much of the cutting-edge research in reverse aging focuses on the mitochondria as the key to longevity. It's become pretty clear that mitochondria health is essential for cognitive strength and our peak cognitive performance demands peak mitochondria conditioning. Yes, the connection is that essential.

As the "CEO of you", positive relationships with these departments are crucial in creating forward momentum toward your goals. It is paramount that in your pursuit of financial reward you do not underestimate the importance of a properly functioning body. Just look at the health transformations of Mark Zuckerberg and Jeff Bezos who have come to understand that optimal body function is key to continued financial performance.

Something I read recently that I found interesting is someone back tested a basket of stocks picked solely on the basis of the health behaviour of the CEO. He called it the Deadlift ETF and it focuses on companies run by people who either lift heavy, engage in deep cardio, or both. The fictional fund when back tested over four years outperformed the S&P 500 by 140 per cent. We need to enlarge our scope of inputs when discussing "wealth" accumulation.

CHAPTER 6

PAYING ATTENTION TO PAYING ATTENTION

So, you isn't the entire you. The microbes in your gut are trying to steer the bus. Epigenetic changes, even those from trauma you may not have experienced firsthand, are influencing your cells. An ancient bacterium, the mitochondria, functions as both an essential power provider and operator of each of your cells. What else? Well, what you think is you—your consciousness—relies on its workers to work.

New research into how consciousness emerges and our cells communicate with each other and process information has revealed—surprise surprise—that consciousness depends on the very cells that we are made of. Our consciousness emerges as the energy flowing within us is utilized across trillions of cells in our body, brain, and nervous system. Working together, our plasma membranes and mitochondria process and share information in a distributed system creating the biological supercomputer that is us.

At the root of all life lies a fundamental truth: Even the simplest cells possess a form of awareness. This isn't the self-reflective consciousness we associate with humanity but a primal ability to sense, respond, and adapt to their environment. This cellular awareness—the drive to survive, repair, and reproduce—is the seed from which consciousness began.

Each of these cells, with their primitive awareness, is capable of contributing to "your" awareness. When enough cells light up together in synchronized patterns with sufficient intensity, they create what we experience as conscious awareness. This isn't a top-down spotlight controlled by a central operator, but rather a bottom-up emergence of cellular consciousness that spreads like waves across cellular networks. Our most active brain regions start to illuminate and act like light bulbs as they cluster and communicate to create our conscious experience.

At the heart of this revolutionary understanding are two crucial players: the cellular membrane—our sophisticated boundary with the world—and the mitochondria—our cellular power plants. This is the fundamental duo which makes consciousness possible. The membrane, with its complex array of proteins and ion channels, acts as both sentinel and communicator. It maintains precise electrical gradients that allow cells to sense and respond to their environment. Meanwhile, mitochondria don't just provide energy—they orchestrate the amplitude and frequency of cellular signaling that directs our conscious experience.

This crucial partnership started over one billion years ago when mitochondria began working in a symbiotic relationship with simple cells and their plasma membranes. Mitochondria became the cell's powerhouses, processing energy with remarkable efficiency through oxidative phosphorylation, a process far superior to the anaerobic methods that had come before. Our current cognitive complexity is the result of a billion years of evolution since this first partnership.

This energy revolution was a game changer. With a reliable and abundant energy supply, cells could support larger genomes, allowing them to create more sophisticated proteins and processes. The door to multicellularity opened, and life took on new dimensions. Specialized tissues emerged, including the nervous systems that would one day give rise to complex thought and emotion.

The human brain, which most people consider our seat of consciousness, is one of the most energy-demanding organs, consuming about 20 per cent of the body's energy despite its small size. Such an energy-demanding organ could never have been possible without the mitochondria powering every synapse, thought, and memory.

But mitochondria do far more than just energy production. They are active participants in cellular signaling, influencing growth, stress responses, and even neural plasticity—the brain's ability to adapt and learn. Their production of reactive oxygen species (ROS) has driven evolutionary adaptations, pushing life to innovate and overcome challenges. Even their unique genetic material, mitochondrial DNA, plays a role in this story, interacting with nuclear DNA to shape traits critical for survival and higher brain function.

So, when we marvel at the human mind's ability to dream, reason, and reflect, we are witnessing the culmination of over a billion years of evolution—an ascent that began with the simplest cellular awareness and was accelerated by the unyielding power of mitochondria. They are the unsung heroes of our conscious existence, the energy engines that fueled life's bold leap from simple survival to the intricate functioning of human thought.

Consider what happens when you walk down a busy street. Your cellular membranes are constantly detecting environmental changes—temperature, pressure, chemical signals—while mitochondria modulate the energy needed to process this information. When something important occurs, like a speeding car approaching, it's not a central control that sounds the alarm. Instead, clusters of cells across your body create synchronized patterns of activity, their membranes and mitochondria working in concert to elevate this information to conscious awareness.

In this new way of thinking, the subconscious mind is a vast network of cellular intelligence, where every cell contributes to decision-making through its membrane-mitochondria partnership.

Your cells are constantly processing information, making decisions, and influencing your awareness without requiring top-down conscious control. This explains why you might sense danger before consciously recognizing it, or why certain memories can trigger physical responses before reaching conscious awareness.

What makes this way of thinking so revolutionary is its explanation of how consciousness emerges from cellular activity. When cellular membranes detect important signals, their mitochondria adjust energy production and signaling patterns. These changes ripple through cellular networks, creating waves of synchronized activity. When enough cells join this synchronization, their collective activity becomes strong enough to enter conscious awareness—like a wave of cellular energy spreading through the body.

This understanding transforms how we view decision-making and attention. Your choices aren't made by "executive function" merely in the brain; they emerge from the collective wisdom of our vastly complex cellular networks, each cell contributing to the process. When you make a decision, it's the result of countless cellular conversations, with membranes detecting and transmitting signals while mitochondria modulate the energy and frequency of these communications.

By understanding consciousness as an emergent property of cellular activity, we can better optimize human performance. Healthy cellular membranes and efficient mitochondria don't just improve energy levels—they enhance our capacity for consciousness itself. This explains why factors like nutrition, sleep, and stress management have such profound effects on our awareness and decision-making abilities.

THE POWER OF CELLULAR ATTENTION

Understanding this cellular foundation of consciousness helps us make better choices about where we direct our attention. Instead of fighting against our biology, we can work with it. When we feel anxious or distracted, we're experiencing the collective response of our cellular networks. These responses aren't random—they're based on sophisticated cellular intelligence evolved over billions of years.

Consider this: When you feel inexplicably drawn to or repelled by something, it's often your cellular networks detecting patterns that your conscious mind hasn't yet recognized. Your cells, through their membrane receptors and mitochondrial signaling, are processing information far more quickly and comprehensively than your conscious mind ever could. Feelings are messages between cells that evolved out of necessity for cells in multicellular organisms to cooperate. Cells use feelings to signal and influence the actions of their entire organism. Whether we choose to focus on our feelings or not, they still emerge from different body regions and influence our decision-making in a huge way.

Instead of trying to force our attention through willpower alone, we can support our cellular health through proper nutrition, movement, and energy management. This creates the conditions for optimal cellular communication, which facilitates clarity of mind and deep focus.

QUESTIONS FOR CELLULAR REFLECTION

When we feel our attention being pulled in certain directions, we might ask ourselves: "What are my cells trying to tell me? Is this cellular network response based on current reality or stored patterns? How can I support my cellular health to make clearer decisions"?

This isn't about giving up control—it's about understanding where our control really lies. By supporting our cellular health through lifestyle choices, managing our energy systems, and respecting our body's signals, we can create conditions for optimal attention and awareness.

THE HARD OR NOT-SO-HARD PROBLEM OF CONSCIOUSNESS

From the moment you feel tired, hungry, or in pain, you're experiencing something remarkable—the direct language of your cells.

What philosophers have long called the "hard problem of consciousness"—understanding how physical processes create subjective experiences—becomes elegantly simple when we recognize that feelings themselves are the biological communication system that evolved to keep complex organisms alive.

Consider fatigue: Rather than being a mysterious sensation added to physical processes, the feeling of tiredness *is* the cellular distress signal itself. When billions of cells need resources or rest, they communicate this need through an intricate network of mitochondria—our cellular power plants. This network creates what we experience as consciousness, not as some emergent mystery, but as a biological necessity for multicellular survival.

As organisms became more complex, cells needed sophisticated ways to share information about their needs and status. What we call consciousness—our inner experience of feelings, sensations, and awareness—is simply this cellular communication system at work. Every subjective experience, from the sharp sting of a paper cut to the warmth of happiness, represents vital information being shared across vast networks of cells.

This perspective eliminates the traditional mind-body divide by showing that consciousness isn't something added to physical processes—it is the process itself. Just as a cell's distress signal isn't separate from its need for resources, our subjective experiences aren't separate from our biology. They are the fundamental language of life, evolved over billions of years to ensure our survival through cellular cooperation.

THE PATH FORWARD

In the end, developing a clear sense of consciousness and improving ability to focus isn't about fighting our biology but working with it. We are not just our conscious thoughts, but the living expression of cellular intelligence refined through evolution. By understanding and supporting this cellular foundation of consciousness, we can make better choices about where we direct our precious attention. Most importantly, we can make conscious efforts to train ourselves to invest our attention by focusing on activities that make us smarter and happier.

This understanding gives us a new kind of freedom—not the freedom to override our biology, but the wisdom to work with it. When we align our conscious goals with our cellular intelligence, we create the conditions for peak performance and clearer awareness. It's about living not just from what rises to consciousness, but from harnessing the deep wisdom of our cellular networks while taking steps to train our cells to adjust priorities and improve their teamwork.

CHAPTER 7

PATTERNS YOU SEE

THERE IS A BIOLOGICAL IMPERATIVE IN FINDING PATTERNS. Newborns can recognize their mother's face and voice within hours, showing that some pattern-recognition abilities are innate. Infants as young as a few months old begin to notice predictable events, like the appearance of their parents or the regularity of feeding, which helps them make sense of their world.

Early brain development relies heavily on pattern recognition. For instance, language acquisition depends on a child's ability to detect phonetic patterns in spoken language. Babies start picking up on sounds, syllable patterns, and tones that will later help them understand and produce language.

And it's deep-rooted: Early humans had to spot predator tracks, dangerous weather cues, or poisonous plants based on recurring shapes, sounds, or environmental patterns. The brain evolved to find these connections, rewarding quick pattern detection with survival. Pattern recognition is also crucial for identifying opportunities, like finding consistent food sources, water, or shelter. So, how does the brain reinforce patterns it likes and punish patterns it doesn't like?

DOPAMINE

Dopamine is often called the "reward chemical" because it reinforces pleasurable experiences, but it also strengthens the brain's focus on patterns that predict rewards. When a person recognizes a pattern that leads to a desired outcome—such as food, social recognition, or success—dopamine release in the brain makes the experience rewarding and encourages repetition of the behaviour. This reward system helps the brain prioritize and learn from beneficial patterns, improving survival by helping us remember and seek out rewarding patterns, like locating food sources or forming social bonds.

Dopamine strengthens learning by increasing plasticity, or adaptability, in neural circuits involved in memory formation. When we detect a pattern, especially one that is novel or significant, dopamine levels spike, reinforcing the memory of the experience. This helps the brain solidify and recall patterns more effectively in the future. For example, if a person learns that certain clouds predict a rainstorm, dopamine can enhance the brain's memory of this pattern, making it easier to remember and recognize in the future. This mechanism ensures that we pay attention to patterns that could signal important changes, like shifts in social dynamics or environmental dangers. High dopamine levels help sustain focus on these patterns until they are understood and integrated.

When dopamine levels rise, they increase our curiosity and drive to explore. This is especially relevant to pattern recognition because curiosity often leads us to seek out new patterns, test hypotheses, and make discoveries. This intrinsic motivation to explore and understand enhances our ability to identify new patterns and predict outcomes, contributing to learning and innovation.

Dopamine can be the "carrot", but it also can be the "stick"; when the brain predicts a pattern that doesn't lead to the anticipated reward, dopamine levels drop, signaling that the pattern was incorrect. This allows for refinement and learning, adjusting the brain's pattern-recognition system. Dopamine neurons also play a role in what's known as "reward prediction error"—they increase or decrease dopamine release depending on whether an outcome is better, worse, or as expected. When there's a positive reward prediction error (when something is more rewarding than expected), dopamine levels rise, signaling that the brain has encountered something new and significant. This mechanism helps fine-tune our recognition of patterns by reinforcing those that are meaningful or predictive of positive outcomes and adjusting expectations when patterns don't deliver the expected results. This is key in learning to distinguish true patterns from noise or coincidence.

Pattern recognition is also crucial to investment success. So, is there a hack to conscript the existing dopamine system into serving beneficial pattern recognition for financial analysis? Short answer is yes.

My maternal grandparents immigrated to Canada from Finland in the 1900s. Investigating my Finnish heritage, I have realized that my ancestors were nomadic hunter-gathers who—from a very early-on stage of my lineage—chose the path less taken. They chose—repeatedly—the less-used path which led them to positive dopamine rewards (probably because it resulted in more prey being successfully found and hunted) and so they repeated the behaviour until they found themselves on the small sliver of land which is now Finland. There is more I have inherited I imagine, like the distrust of the mob and wanting to go it alone, but for now let's keep to the hunter-gatherer reward system I have—at first by accident and now intentionally—tapped into.

This "prey to be found on the path less taken" wiring was reinforced by my father (probably because of his father and his father before him) by the stories he would tell. I remember so vividly one poem he used to read to me, "The Road Not Taken" by Robert Frost:

Two roads diverged in a yellow wood,
And sorry I could not travel both
And be one traveler, long I stood
And looked down one as far as I could
To where it bent in the undergrowth;

Then took the other, as just as fair,
And having perhaps the better claim,
Because it was grassy and wanted wear;
Though as for that the passing there
Had worn them really about the same,

And both that morning equally lay
In leaves no step had trodden black.
Oh, I kept the first for another day!
Yet knowing how way leads on to way,
I doubted if I should ever come back.

I shall be telling this with a sigh
Somewhere ages and ages hence:
Two roads diverged in a wood, and I—
I took the one less traveled by,
And that has made all the difference.

I am instantly filled with the visualization of an overgrown path just barely discernible but baring such opportunity. My father further grooved this wiring into me, and it wasn't so surprising I guess that this wiring jumped from animal prey to the big-game-hunting thrill I found hunting opportunities in the financial markets.

MY FIRST MAJOR MACRO THESIS: WHERE DOES THE "BIG GAME" LIVE?

I am going to talk about my contrarian style and what signs I look for when hunting for 10x financial opportunities. But first we need to get the lay of the land. Nearly everything runs in a cyclical pattern and the more I studied history, the more that became apparent to me. Of course the natural world runs fundamentally in a cyclical pattern. And not just nature, but there are political cycles, fashion cycles, and of course financial investment cycles. Investment cycles of all sorts can have vastly different lengths, and some investors even like to track seasonality where there's patterns of trends throughout the year for various stock sectors.

My initial macro studies had me focused on trying to predict how the tech boom-to-bubble-and-bust cycle would play out. Researching historic bubbles, South Sea, Tulip Mania, the crash of '29, gold and silver peaking in 1980, Japanese stock, and the real estate market bubble of 1990 provided many insights and shaped my entire focus and dictated the investment style I ultimately developed for the long term.

I came to believe that—regardless of government or central bank efforts—we will inevitably develop financial bubbles in different sectors that result in booms and busts to varying degrees. This creates extremely dangerous times for our jobs, our businesses, and our financial health. Our physical health is also placed at risk as our economic problems affect our freedom and stress levels. Financial calamities also typically lead to big swings in political ideologies with huge ramifications for actual freedom, free markets, taxation, and property ownership.

The most famous and historic bubbles that took place prior to the 1900s often triggered long periods of a depressed economy and political unrest. Many revolutions in history resulted directly from the bursting of a major economic bubble that triggered widespread financial loss, high unemployment, periods of huge deflation quickly followed by rampant inflation and a breakdown in the social order. One thing in history that's for certain is that when masses of people are starving, they riot and overthrow governments. Also, when nearly everyone falls into financial ruin, with a failing banking system, they riot and typically lynch both their political leaders and the bankers.

Which brings me to the history of central banking. There's no doubt in my mind that the central banking system was founded by insiders in the banking industry so that if all else fails, the banking industry is protected. Never lose sight of this fact as we carry on with my macro thesis and this entire book. It's a core principle we must be wary of. Our modern central banking system was developed and founded by a group of bankers and adopted by our political leaders of the time. The year 1913 saw the formation of the USA's Federal Reserve Bank and soon after a huge expansion in credit followed. Up to this point major global currencies like the British pound and the US dollar were backed by gold reserves and convertible into gold and both governments held substantial reserves.

History had been extremely unkind to governments and bankers that dared to experiment with fractional reserve banking. In fact, every single experiment in history with paper money that wasn't backed by a commodity has failed with the currency losing all value and becoming abandoned. Even the fall of Rome can be attributed to excess government spending and budget deficits leading to currency devaluation through debasement that resulted in a breakdown in commerce.

Today, governments continually run greater and greater deficits willed on by a voting public that doesn't want to pay taxes. An ever-growing larger percentage of the population came to specialize in lobbying our government for handouts and bailouts. The banking system has increasingly found more ways to employ greater leverage and create more money while lobbying for less regulation so they can create even more money all the while lining their pockets with excessive amounts of it. This combo has repeatedly produced major bubbles in one sector of the economy after another as bankers and stockbrokers enjoyed huge profits from funneling a flow of newly created money into various sectors while singing their long-term praises. Bubble periods see a giant misallocation of capital and when it's finally clear to all that the sector isn't going to provide profitable returns, it implodes right after the last dimwit available is sucked in to buy the top. This triggers a cry for help and of course money printing and interest rate slashing.

So, I think we need to discuss what happened in 2000, post Y2K, to help us predict the road ahead. As well, I refined the overall macro view and developed what I call an "intrinsic energy principle of investing", the cornerstone of my long-term repeatable investment strategy. This review might inspire you to study resource investing and prepare to repeatedly profit from its cyclicality over a long-term cycle-based investment horizon.

THE INTRINSIC ENERGY PRINCIPLE OF INVESTING: ZEROING IN ON THE HUNT

The crux of this way of looking at stocks and sectors is to focus not on the existing or potential profits in nominal terms. Instead, we need to consider if the profit margins appear sustainable in real terms and are more likely to grow or decline. The underlying principle of what makes the cut in terms of investment criteria is clarity on the business's competitive advantage in terms of return on energy invested, energy saved, or energy produced.

When a business has a serious energy cost advantage for making its products it typically coincides with that margin being both sustainable against competitors and versus inflation. In some cases, we may find that margins may improve with energy cost inflation making the investment extremely attractive in times that we expect it to rise or when we seek to balance out other risks in our portfolio.

Take any commodity producer in the resource sector. When breaking down the operating cost into its various components we can see that nearly everything can be somewhat related to energy as well as compared to its competitors. Whether underground or open pit mining, there's a cost to access and move ore. By studying a wide range of active mines, we discover the wide range of costs and the reasons why some may be dramatically higher than others. The harder the rock is to extract, the more costs go up as energy consumption increases with effort. Depth, overburden, seam thickness, slope, mining method, and location are all huge factors. Costs can all be estimated with the help of skilled knowledgeable analysts and engineers. You find this sort of information in dedicated resource books, annual reports of various mining companies, and feasibility studies, as well as analyst reports. For now, just understand that each of the components that factors into production cost relates to energy consumption.

When we consider the intrinsic value of the mining company's ore on a per-tonne basis versus all-in production costs, we begin to get a picture of margin potential versus peers. When we look across an entire sector, we then gain a better understanding of what the average costs are as well as the overall range. Obviously, the lower the cost the higher the margin. But also remember that since all resources are generally super cyclical market prices are going to oscillate from highs to lows and margins will correspondingly explode higher, generating wild upswings in the value of a company or possibly evaporate, driving some high-cost producers into bankruptcy especially ones with debt.

That volatility that seems to always attract me is probably the main reason I was so attracted to the resource sector. It's one of the few sectors that behaves over the long run with somewhat of a cyclical certainty and often offers huge mispricing of both risk and reward that informed speculators can capitalize on. It's vilified as being high-volatility and high-risk by people who haven't taken the time to really develop a resource investment strategy that only focuses on the very long term and therefore delivers unparalleled risk-reward opportunities. Developing expertise in resource investing in this fashion will surely result in an investor being able to clearly and confidently identify many outstanding investments over a multidecade investment time horizon.

A very general rule of thumb for most commodities is that operating costs run around half of the total cost of production with up-front capital costs making up the other half. There's great variance in this ratio across commodities and mining methods and I'm using this fifty-fifty ratio to help illustrate a point. Projects with this sort of cost split require a significant up-front investment to just build a mine relative to its operating costs. Let's assume we are talking about a mine that has a ten-year mining life. That would mean that the capital cost would be amortized over the ten years such that the CapEx would be around five times that of the total yearly all in mining cost (without getting into discount rates and interest expenses or maintenance CapEx). The point I'm trying to illustrate is that to build a mine there's a big up-front risk that must be taken and the companies and investors taking that risk need to believe that commodity prices will stay high enough to cover operating costs with ample margin to pay back the initial investment building a mine.

As a result, once a production shortage develops in a mining sector, prices tend to rise significantly and need to stay high to encourage CapEx investment to develop new mines. Again, all this CapEx can be related to an energy investment in the development of the mine. Cost of the equipment that's needed relates to the energy that was used to make the equipment. All raw materials used in the project relate to energy costs that have been sunk in them. The entire investment into CapEx and OpEx (capital expenses and operational expenses) can therefore be seen in terms of a massive energy investment.

Now let's focus more on the cyclicality and range of the price movements as the mining sector moves from boom to bust. Once a sector ramps up in response to good margins it's just a matter of time until oversupply is reached and prices start to fall.

During major economic crashes prices can dip to extreme levels and we saw the greatest example of this during the oil market's COVID-19-related crash of 2020. Prices fell to $0 per barrel because there was so much oversupply that there was actually no oil storage available, and producers were forced to shut in producing wells. It was a major anomaly and presented one of the greatest times to buy oil and gas stocks in recent memory. They were simply being thrown away in a liquidity crisis. We shouldn't expect to get many opportunities like that again in a lifetime. What is more normal is for prices to fall around the average operating costs for a given resource sector.

Amazingly, time and again, all these industries inevitably get this depressed. In bad times of oversupply, nobody cares about what you spent on a mine. Resource companies are reluctant to seriously curtail operating production. They seek to avoid laying off employees and angering local communities and governments. As long as they can make some money on a cash basis versus operating cost, they typically continue producing. Only the highest cost operating mines shut down in cyclical depressions and often only due to bankruptcy.

Analyze any long-term commodity chart and dig through its industry news during the lows. Bottoms are always correlated with depressing headlines reporting layoffs, losses, closures, production cutbacks, bankruptcies, and lawsuits. When you look at commodity price peaks you'll see the opposite: record profits, dividend increases, big bonuses, charitable giving, award ceremonies, ribbon cutting, labor shortages, mergers and acquisitions with competing bidders, and large takeover premiums.

During the swing from cycle highs to cycle lows, companies with hundreds of millions and sometimes billions of dollars sunk in mining construction costs, trade down to modest multiples of net operating cash flow. Pessimistic stock investors give up, believing high prices aren't going to be coming back anytime soon, and that the risk of further failures is still high. Nevertheless, when commodity prices swing from lows back to highs, valuations come surging back with most depressed stocks easily rallying 10x, and fortunes are made as some have been known to rally 100x or more. The kind of numbers that my "hunter-gatherer" reward center loves.

This is the pattern I uncovered in the late 1990s during my research into stock market history and my hunt for repeatably mispriced risk-reward opportunities. The timing was nearly perfect to capitalize on the knowledge I began building. The resource sector had been in a twenty-year bear market exhibiting all the characteristics of a major bottom. On top of it all, we had an explosion of growth just starting as China was emerging as a global manufacturing hub and India was ramping up its services and manufacturing sectors. Many emerging markets with huge populations engaged in pro-growth economic reforms and recovered well from the 1997 Asian crisis. The East with half the world's population was finally hungry to join the West in its pursuit of a major consumerist culture. All commodities would need to see a big ramp-up in production to meet the emerging demand.

Gold was sub $300 per ounce, silver around $4 per ounce, and I fell in love with both.

I was supremely confident that the tech bubble was going to burst, leading to rate cutting and more money printing. I saw the rise of China and India as being great for gold. When I considered the average production cost for silver, I drew the conclusion that it must go up and go up a lot. From my new way of considering value, I figured buying silver at $4 was sort of like getting the silver for free, with me only paying for delivery from underground to my home. Miners at that time were willing to mine, refine, and sell their silver resources for their cost of production and sometimes less as most miners were cash flow negative. I viewed stockpiling silver as being a permanent call on energy. After all, as discussed above, the operating cost could be broken down entirely to an intrinsic energy cost. So, if the production cost was all energy, and I believed energy costs would be going much higher, then the price of silver must rise at least to match, eventually producing mines would be exhausted and once again the massive up-front cost to build a mine would become a factor. Nobody was going to be building new mines at $4 silver, that was for sure. I felt I had a sure double within a decade, and a chance thing could get crazy again and that 1980 historical silver price of $50 per ounce sure sounded like fun.

I've spent a lot of time here covering the Intrinsic Energy Principle of Investing from only a resource perspective. But it applies to many industries and sectors. When a new technology is developed that saves people time and money, you can consider this in terms of energy being saved and the sustainability of margin. If dynamics of that energy savings is such that its likely to go up over time, then the margins are very sustainable. Further, when a product is substitutable for another and is much cheaper in terms of energy costs you can expect a shift to take place and margins to be maintained by the newcomer and lost by the inefficient one.

Sifting through down cycle, less sexy, headline-less sectors rife with bad news might sound like a dead end, but this is exactly where the big game on the path not taken, live. We have a system that encourages bubbles. These bubbles are full of feel-good triggers. They make everyone feel smart and give consistent dopamine hits because the market makes everyone money. Until it doesn't of course. But when a sector is bubbling, it feels good biologically speaking to join in.

In turn the bubbling sector attracts money away from sectors that should be getting investment. This exacerbates the risk-reward on mispriced stock. I go where the crowds are not, because I know when one sector is irrationally attracting capital interest there is another sector that is irrationally losing capital interest and that is the sector I want to be hunting in. On the Road Not Taken. But being where others aren't isn't enough. There are behavioural traits I have noticed that seem to be a common thread through successful investors.

EMOTIONAL INTELLIGENCE

By studying history and ways other people have made money you begin to understand the emotions of a broad range of market participants. You'll see there are always peaks and valleys as stocks move in and out of a long-term bull or bear market. Emotional intelligence will help you through the short-term market swings, the greed, the fear, and the excitement that drives the market. I used to get caught up in the excitement, but I've rewired myself to take a step back. Instead, I look for the short-term tops and bottoms created by all that excitement.

I've trained myself to buy my pain and sell my joy. That approach feels more productive to me. Taking at least some profits after a powerful up move when I'm feeling great gives me the opportunity to invest after a big correction, buying back the stocks I love most. This allows me to stay focused and positive during the downturns, acquiring more stock and achieving higher returns. Exercising this patience allows you to outperform the market and also rotate capital effectively between overheating sectors to underperforming ones that might present better risk-reward in the moment.

MAKE MISTAKES EARLY AND QUICKLY

I've mentioned the importance of starting small and building on successes when starting out and I suggest journaling to help identify your potential blind spots. Best to flush out mistakes you're making while paper trading or investing with small dollars.

Learn the skills I'm going to teach you here. Otherwise, you may be making knee-jerk reactions to market swings or just as bad, maybe worse, you might avoid making decisions, altogether abandoning your portfolio when it needs you most.

DECISIVE BEATS IMPULSIVE

You must be decisive, but your decisions must be based on facts, not emotions or "feelings". You need the knowledge and skills to make quick decisions that make sense. It takes time to develop the skills and mastery to make fast, insightful decisions, so we must adjust our investments horizon that matches our financial expertise. Consider researching investments that appear to be good sectors in five or ten years, not five or ten days, weeks, or months. Some investors prefer to model out a company's potential earnings in detail while others are fine with more loosely based approximations. I've generally found that if I can't do basic math in my head and be confident that the stock is very cheap, then most likely, the prospects of the company are too marginal and there are too many unknowns and risks in their business model. A lot of things can and generally do go wrong in the business world. Considering the vast number of companies out there we can choose from, it makes sense to focus on looking for massive opportunities to outperform. If I don't see that potential in a company or sector, I'm not going to make the investment.

PATIENCE IS YOUR TOP EARNER

This can mean the inability to wait for opportunities, or lacking the focus to even plan, or not taking time to identify and only invest in the true risk-reward ratio sweet spots that result from your analysis. Too often people in the trading office adopted the mindset of, "I'm here, and I'm a trader, so I need to be trading". You must be patient and decide not only what to invest in but when to invest in it. I have investment horizons for as long as ten years. Sometimes an investment window moves up due to market changes and I modify my plan. Sometimes it pays off more quickly than I expect. It doesn't always go the way I planned, but I am very patient, constantly reviewing the situation to see what's changed and how the risk to reward is evolving. For fund managers, the tendency is to remain fully invested but many of the greats have proven time and again that they are willing to go to 20 or 30 per cent cash when they don't like the markets and then go all in following a correction. This is rarely done but is extremely effective and how I personally manage my own money. Sometimes I've gone higher than 50 per cent cash and waited for a year or more. Like Buffett, I prefer waiting for a fat pitch to hit at this stage in my investing.

REASON & RULES OVER EGO & OVERCONFIDENCE

A massive problem for traders is overconfidence or just plain ego. I saw these many times with highly educated professionals like doctors and lawyers as well as seasoned money managers. They think because they are smart at one thing, they're smart at everything, and that attitude bites them in the butt. The most dangerous times are always when you've been on a great run. People let their guard down and act out of hubris. Both in business and in fund management this sometimes results from becoming overwhelmed by success-based growth. Capital starts pouring into a fund because of past performance and a manager is reluctant to admit they should close their strategy to new investment and instead finds themselves cutting corners on due diligence in order to put capital to work in a timely fashion.

For high-growth businesses, the problem manifests as they take on too many clients or commit to too high a growth such that quality is impacted leading to customer dissatisfaction and major setbacks. The best money and business managers have enough self-doubt to check and double-check themselves before pulling the trigger over expanding or making sure every buy or sell always checks all the boxes. Too much confidence can lead you to convince yourself that you're always right, when in fact, you are not seeing all the facts. I've seen people get tunnel vision into a particular sector and flat out want to avoid looking at the negative developments as they arise. That obsession led them to make bad decisions. Others' focus might become much too myopic, and they fall in love with a great company in a doomed sector that takes it down with it.

DETAILED TRADING PLAN OVER INCONSISTENT DISCIPLINE

You have to make a trading plan and stick to it. If you keep changing it up and aren't rule based, then you're typically just having a lucky streak and aren't learning anything. Maybe the market keeps bailing you out, but that doesn't make you a good investor. For people who break their investment plans, it's only a matter of time before they get whacked. Remember if you break your investment plan, then you essentially are operating without a plan altogether. Often, this leads to being hurt badly after developing bad habits, like averaging down when they shouldn't. They end up having a few consecutive big losses that wipe them out, occasionally destroying their savings and their reputation. I've seen this happen over and over again. It's also been amazing to me how many good analysts I've gotten to know that are actually terrible investors in their own portfolios.

They're good at playing the game of being a broker or even a money manager where they must follow a mandate. Even accountants that have incredible structure and processes in the workplace often have disastrously undisciplined personal investment records. Sector analysts fall into the trap of thinking they know a sector so well that they're always going to make money in it. Then, when their sector tanks, it takes them down and all their money with it. Due to the addition of career risk, many have been known to personally invest in a countercyclical fashion to the fund they manage. I once interviewed a top fund manager that owned no stocks at all personally; they kept all their own money in real estate. We didn't end up hiring them as I couldn't help but feel they didn't have enough personal alignment with their fund strategy.

THICK SKIN

Some people are good traders, but if they lose, they can't handle it. Maybe sometimes we need to take a day off from trading to recover or even a holiday to free our minds and reset. But many novice investors suffer losses they can't forgive themselves for and quit for good. You have to be able to overcome losses, pick yourself up, and keep going. The worst response is revenge trading, where people think they can make back what they lost by getting bigger or more aggressive. This nearly always results in bad decisions and results in greater losses. Like doubling down on a bet at a casino after losing. Chasing the money is never good.

A good friend of mine once used trading analytics to determine that if he lost money in the morning he consistently lost even more in the afternoon. So, he made it a rule that if he lost in the morning, he would take the afternoon off. To have continued reliable success you need to be focused and in the right frame of mind. Avoid emotional regret and figure out how your process failed and fix it.

FOREVER THE STUDENT OVER BEING A MASTER

You need to be able to be good at tech, especially now with AI and other analytic software tools. If you're not willing to take on technology and use the latest analytical software and filters, you'll be at a major disadvantage against all the people who are learning it and using it. This includes not just trading-related software but researching tools and modeling and accounting software. If I was a young ambitious investor, I would focus on mastering AI and new technology tools with a goal of gaining the underserved prestige and authority that comes with it, as author Neil Postman wrote about in his famous book *Technopoly*.[2] Bringing strong tech skills to any industry is a smart approach. But "forever the student" goes beyond tech.

Some investors think they know everything they need to know, and they stop pursuing new knowledge. If you want to succeed, you have to keep educating yourself about the markets and looking for change before it arrives to surprise you. Dedication to continuous learning isn't just good for your portfolio; it's also good for your brain and your health. The best investment you can make is in yourself and your continuing education.

When I was younger, I was geared toward short-term gratification. I didn't think too much about the future, in part because I grew up planning to go into business with my father when he retired. I was developing construction skills and thought I had a financial backer as a father, so I never took my education seriously. I also spent everything I earned on cars, vacations, and whatever else I wanted at the moment. But, when my father's health deteriorated culminating with his death in my early twenties, I found myself a broke university dropout who was disillusioned and depressed. I had to retrain myself, evolve, stop spending, and start studying. I had to develop skills that would help me make money. I had to regroup and rewire myself. I learned to live within my means for the first time and then learned how to invest.

Some people are led to day trading and full-time investing because they value wealth, or they want to be in the money business, and they think trading and investing is a good way to pursue their financial interests and goals. Some people are attracted to money epigenetically. They're drawn to it, and it excites them. Some people think greed is good, and although that philosophy can be debated it sure does buy freedom.

---

2   Neil Postman, *Technopoly: The Surrender of Culture to Technology* (Vintage Books, 1993), 9.

People can make a lot of money as professional investors and the ones that do typically really enjoy the work required. To become a pro, you need to also love the process of learning how to trade and invest.

Making a commitment to continual learning and strategy around investing and managing your finances is a big step. But I want to drive home the message that if you're not going to be willing to really dig in and do the work, then it's best to seek out advisory services from a quality broker you trust, while determining that they are true students of the market and that they will be diligent in their advisory role when safeguarding your capital. The dollar cost averaging, broad based investing approach via low fee index funds is also a good fall-back approach as well as investing early in life so that you have the maximum time to experience compounded portfolio growth.

But I'm guessing that you picked up this book to learn more than that standard advice. More likely, you seek superior performance. You're willing to try to use your own logic and reasoning to help navigate your investment allocations to manage your risk and hopefully gain greater rewards. This all will follow as you continually make compounding investment in yourself. You can't just dabble here and there expecting to get rich or even make a quick buck. Take heart though, if you don't have the right wiring and mindset to be a trader, you can develop it. Still, we always have to work to maintain it. Close to thirty years of investing and I still find myself making occasional errors in judgment and rule breaking. This despite knowing better and having worked so hard to educate myself early on so my natural flawed instincts wouldn't ruin me. We are all a continuous work in progress and there is always something new to discover and for that, you need to focus on—first and foremost—what you're not seeing.

PART TWO

DIAGNOSE

Where Is Your Energy Going?

CHAPTER 8

PATTERNS YOU DON'T SEE

EVERYTHING COMES DOWN TO PATTERN RECOGNITION. The best patterns to find are the ones on the path not taken. I have a friend who discovered a pattern that no one is seeing, takes no real effort to deploy, and is giving him a 35 per cent annualized return. I wish I could tell you more about it, but if everyone started doing it, the opportunity he found would disappear. What I can tell you is how to go about finding ones you can use. The market is always changing and opportunities open up and disappear all the time.

Pattern recognition is an indispensable tool when investing. It also helps you recognize healthy and not-so-healthy routines you may or may not have. The more "of the whole picture" you can see, the better your analysis—regardless of the subject—will be.

There are more patterns we don't see than do see. Many remain hidden beneath the surface, embedded in our subconscious mind. But—although not consciously aware of them—these hidden patterns have a huge impact on our beliefs, behaviours, and decisions, often without us even realizing it.

So, what exactly is happening? How can we access—consciously—the patterns the subconscious has recognized, noted, and then deemed not important enough to bring into our conscious thought? What should be of concern is that we might not have consciously recognized a pattern, but our subconscious has and it's a pattern that is now influencing our behaviour—possibly to our detriment. Either way, I'd prefer to consciously acknowledge my choices, evaluate the risk-reward of my current behaviour, and properly consider the alternatives.

When an experience or pattern impresses itself deeply enough—through repetition, emotional intensity, or survival instincts—it gets stored in the subconscious. This imprint can influence your behaviour in ways that are often automatic, almost reflexive, and difficult to change without first becoming aware of them. Some pattern impressions are through your experience, whereas others came already built into your operating system.

Your cells are communicating with your ancestors behind your back.

A small refresher on epigenetics: It refers to how your genes can be turned "on" or "off" by your environment, experiences, and even those of your ancestors. Trauma, stress, and emotional experiences leave a biological imprint, impacting which genes are expressed without altering the DNA itself. This inheritance can manifest as patterns of fear, anxiety, or even self-sabotaging behaviours that seem to come from nowhere.

Epigenetic influences carry the effects of our ancestors' experiences into our subconscious, shaping us before we're even born. If your grandparents faced extreme hardship, your genes might be "programmed" to stay on high alert, ready for stress and danger. This genetic inheritance can form the basis of subconscious patterns that don't seem to fit with your life's circumstances but still affect how you react to the world.

These inherited patterns can create a subconscious baseline of anxiety, pessimism, or hypervigilance, guiding your thoughts without you even realizing it.

When we carry this genetic and emotional baggage, it can prevent our ability to fully focus and function at full capacity. Imagine trying to see a new pattern while constantly experiencing a background noise of inherited anxieties. You don't care so much about what you are focusing on if there is this constant buzzing sound distracting you.

This "noise" we can't ignore or tune out crowds our minds, making it difficult to notice or understand the patterns in our lives. By becoming aware of these inherited influences, you can begin to unpack and question them. Simple self-enquiry exercises, like asking, "Is this fear truly mine"? can help create space between inherited patterns and your conscious mind, weakening the hold these patterns have over you.

If epigenetics is a distracting buzzing noise, trauma is the deafening fire alarm that can overwhelm everything. Trauma doesn't only leave scars on our minds; it rewires them. Our brains, after trauma, can become hyperaware of certain types of threats, making us vigilant and reactive to triggers that remind us of past pain.

In that way, trauma has a powerful way of encoding itself in the subconscious. When you experience trauma, your brain releases stress hormones that heighten awareness and focus, imprinting the traumatic event into your subconscious as a protective mechanism. These memories and responses are then stored to help you avoid similar threats in the future.

However, because the subconscious doesn't distinguish between past and present, these trauma-imprinted patterns often get replayed. A childhood fear of abandonment, for example, can lead to subconscious patterns of people-pleasing or anxiety in adult relationships. You may find yourself repeating behaviours—such as avoiding conflict or pushing people away—without knowing why.

When we don't recognize these subconscious patterns, they take up valuable space in the processing power, directing our thoughts and actions without conscious input.

When our minds are caught in a trauma loop, it disrupts our concentration. Think of it like being at a play where the same scene is repeatedly replayed. Trauma can dominate the stage, limiting space for other ideas and insights to take shape. Instead of recognizing patterns in the present, your mind is trapped in patterns of the past, desperately replaying old survival strategies that, though no longer needed, keep you from seeing the present clearly.

YOU'RE THE PROBLEM

There are also patterns which we willfully don't want to see. Cognitive dissonance is the discomfort we feel when our beliefs and actions don't match. It manifests as actual cellular conflict patterns. When beliefs clash with new information or actions, this creates competing signal patterns in cellular networks, triggering stress responses at the cellular level, and cognitive dissonance then becomes an "anti-pattern filter" that keeps you from seeing any ideas that conflict with your self-image.

If recognizing a pattern would force you to confront an uncomfortable truth, your mind will actively avoid it. For example, if you see yourself as a person who values health but repeatedly make choices that go against that belief, you'll feel a tension in your mind. To reduce this discomfort, your brain may downplay the importance of health or rationalize your behaviour. In this way, cognitive dissonance can make you "blind" to patterns that, if seen, could lead to meaningful change. This blindness is protective, keeping your ego safe from the discomfort of change, but it comes at the cost of awareness.

Cognitive dissonance works subtly, protecting us from acknowledging patterns that might be uncomfortable or at odds with our self-concept. If your subconscious holds a belief that contradicts your current behaviour or self-image, cognitive dissonance keeps that belief hidden. For example, if you subconsciously believe that you are unworthy of love, yet consciously believe you deserve fulfilling relationships, you may sabotage your own relationships without understanding why.

Cognitive dissonance operates like a mental gatekeeper, deciding which subconscious patterns are allowed to surface. Only when we consciously choose to explore and confront discomfort can we unlock the potential for these patterns to move from subconscious to conscious awareness. Practicing radical self-honesty and giving yourself permission to feel uncomfortable is the first step to allowing these buried beliefs to rise to the surface where you can begin working with them.

CAN YOU TRUST YOUR GUT?

It might seem strange to link the bacteria in your gut with your ability to recognize patterns, but recent research reveals that your gut biome has a profound influence on your mental health and cognitive function. The gut-brain axis is a complex communication network, with gut bacteria influencing neurotransmitter production, stress responses, and mood regulation.

A disrupted gut biome can lead to increased anxiety, depression, and cognitive fog—all of which impact our ability to focus our attention. When your mind feels foggy or overly anxious, it becomes much harder to notice patterns or make connections. You may feel "stuck" in negative thought patterns, missing out on the big-picture thinking necessary to make meaningful changes.

When your gut health is optimized, it creates a healthier communication channel between the gut and the brain. Your mood improves, mental clarity increases, and the "fog" lifts. This mental clarity gives the subconscious mind space to release old patterns, allowing them to rise into your conscious mind where you can begin examining them. Supporting your gut health through a balanced diet, probiotics, and stress reduction helps create the conditions necessary for subconscious patterns to become accessible.

It's a reservoir of experiences, beliefs, and memories that seeks to protect and guide you. Yet, when left unchecked, it can direct your life from the shadows, leading you into cycles and behaviours that don't serve you. By understanding how patterns migrate from the subconscious to the conscious, you can actively engage with these influences and bring them into the light of your mind's eye. Your subconscious mind is not your enemy unless you consciously let it be.

With practice, patience, and a commitment to self-awareness, you can reshape the patterns that have long directed your life. Each pattern brought into consciousness is a stepping stone toward intentionality, allowing you to live a life directed by your highest self rather than the unseen forces of the past.

For you to do any sort of analysis, it is imperative that you work on removing distortions. Be them inherited or developed, the more clearly you can see "the whole picture" the better you will be able to recognize patterns and have the emotional bandwidth to deal with the ups and downs that invariably come with all aspects of life and finances.

MITOCHONDRIA

When mitochondria are unhealthy, their impaired function can have significant effects on cognitive abilities, including pattern recognition, which is central to how we perceive and make sense of the world. Our brain relies on an interconnected network of neurons to process and integrate information, enabling us to recognize patterns, solve problems, and make decisions. Mitochondria play a crucial role in powering these neurons, providing the energy necessary for efficient brain function. If mitochondria are compromised, the brain's capacity to maintain the synchronization and communication between different areas may be disrupted. This can lead to difficulties in recognizing patterns, as the brain struggles to effectively consolidate and process incoming sensory information.

Over time, this impairment can hinder cognitive flexibility, making it harder to adapt to new situations or anticipate future events based on previous experiences. Ultimately, an unhealthy mitochondrial system can undermine the brain's ability to detect patterns, which is essential for navigating daily life and understanding complex relationships.

CHAPTER 9

UNINSTALLING TRAUMA

I WANT TO DRILL DOWN A BIT ON MY METHODOLOGY. I HAVE applied the same "energy" metric that I use to find financial investments to the research I have done on trying to find the "10x" version of myself. I am trying to maximize the results from the energy that I invest into myself. And so, I want to revisit the motivation–ability axis that B. J. Fogg talks about in *Tiny Habits*.

Investing in motivation is not efficient. There are too many factors that make motivation an unreliable business partner in the venture that is you. It is much better to invest that energy into skill acquisition. So, to maximize energy flow toward my goals, I need to discover and deal with my "energy leakages"—actions that I perform which aren't in the service of my goals. My need to address trauma, epigenetics, gut health, mitochondria optimization is all done in the effort to maximize the efficiencies in acquiring abilities. These abilities in turn increase the efficiencies of turning my energy input into results. It is a positive feedback loop and this "co-vitality spiral" is the most efficient way of achieving results. Regardless of the goal.

My concept of the "energetic investor" is about making you the most efficient version of yourself in turning effort into results. And in that service, I want to briefly talk about how I addressed the "energy leakages" stemming from trauma. Again, this is not a recipe book; I am not telling you to do this therapy or that therapy. I want you to have the tools you need to make informed decisions yourself. I decided that I need to clear up some of the trauma "clutter" that had been occupying space in my subconscious and leading to default to many suboptimal choices in my life without rationally considering my options and taking a better path.

The therapy tool that resonated with me was the Internal Family Systems therapy (IFS). This is a form of psychotherapy developed by Dr. Richard Schwartz in the 1980s. It is based on the idea that the mind is made up of multiple "parts", or subpersonalities, each with its own feelings, thoughts, and behaviours. These parts can interact with each other in complex ways, sometimes leading to emotional distress or psychological problems.

IFS is grounded in the belief that everyone has a core Self, which is characterized by qualities like calmness, curiosity, compassion, and clarity. The goal of IFS therapy is to help individuals reconnect with their core Self and develop healthier relationships with their internal parts.

In IFS therapy, the vulnerable parts are referred to as the "exiles", or exiled parts we push down and ignore. We hide those parts and defend them with our protective parts. If we're triggered and get upset, our vulnerable, sensitive part hides, allowing the defensive part to step in. The protective part often goes on the attack, maybe by insulting or belittling the trigger, telling it to go away, and getting us to focus on something else so that we don't experience the bad feelings associated with memories that might be triggered.

IFS therapy refers to the protective part as the firefighter. When our exiles, our vulnerable parts, become emotionally hurt or scared, they are triggered to retreat. Then, the protective part steps in to fight the battle, or it sometimes distracts us from whatever's upsetting the exiles.

The firefighter can choose to look at social media or turn on the TV. They grab snacks or pour a drink. Go out for a smoke. That protective part doesn't want us to be sad or upset, and so it soothes us with consumption and other means that deliver chemicals like dopamine, serotonin, and GABA, making us feel better. Maybe if we let the firefighter take over, we tell ourselves, we can forget about those triggers forever.

It was the therapy exercises that made me recognize what my fire-fighter was doing for me, or rather, parts of me. It drove me toward booze and comfort foods. It distracted me with unhealthy activities. For some people, the firefighter drives them toward addictions like gambling, sex, and drugs. They go deeper into more self-destructive behaviour to gain a sense of control over their pain. Our firefighters might protect us in the short-term from uncomfortable issues. Still, we have to recognize when those choices are leading to destructive long-term issues. Smoking, vaping, and even biting your fingernails are signs of the firefighter taking over, but there are extreme mea-sures too, such as cutting, engaging in high-risk behaviours, and even extreme sports.

But most problems don't go away, and those soothing solutions aren't productive. Some leave us with an upset stomach or bloated and chemically unbalanced, and when we really overdo the drinking, hungover. We have accomplished nothing, are no closer to our life's goals, and are in fact even further from them. So now, we feel even worse. Our dopamine and serotonin have been depleted, and we have no energy. Too often I found that I would make plans to do all sorts of great activities only to let the tiredness following late-night cheer dash my morning plans.

It became clear I had clusters of neurons focused on protecting and distracting me from my painful memories. Those clusters were part of my wiring. The firefighter part of me might help me out with com-petitive activities like sports in my personal life and hard work in my professional life. But it was also hurting me with comfort foods, liquor, and an increasingly sedentary lifestyle. At times, my firefighter didn't consider my long-term health, but felt it deserved a break because it was working so hard. It was driving the bus, leading me on a path to weight gain, energy loss, and injury as I continued pursuing sports my body wasn't prepared to handle safely.

I dove into IFS therapy and tried some exercises, including a powerful meditative exercise called the "redo" or "do over" technique. This resulted in a true epiphany moment for me which, although somewhat embarrassing, I would be remiss not to share. It opened the door to understanding many of my behaviours and was the first step toward undoing some early programming errors that were ingrained in me. It was my first step toward wrestling control from the firefighter and empowering my exiled vulnerable part to step forward, enabling the "self" to create balance and prioritize self-care.

Our brains have a hard time distinguishing between memories, visualizations, and even dreams. From a biological standpoint, proper visualization lights up the exact same areas of the brain as "real" memories, and this brain mechanism that makes eyewitness reports so unreliable is the same mechanism that make IFS visualization so effective.

Eyewitness testimony can be unreliable because our memories are reconstructive, not exact recordings. When recalling an event, we can unintentionally mix in details we didn't actually observe, especially when influenced by external suggestions. Even subtle hints, such as misleading questions or images, can alter our recollection. Confidence in our memories doesn't guarantee accuracy, and stress or trauma can distort what we remember. Additionally, when we try to visualize an event, our minds may fill in gaps with false details. These factors show why eyewitness accounts, though compelling, are often unreliable.

The same brain mechanisms that make eyewitness testimony unreliable—such as memory reconstruction, suggestion, and the integration of new information—are also key to the effectiveness of "redo" visualization in Internal Family Systems (IFS) therapy. In both cases, the brain doesn't simply recall events as they happened but reconstructs memories by weaving together past experiences with present emotions and new perspectives. In IFS therapy, "redo" visualization taps into this mechanism to help individuals reframe or reexperience past events from a more empowered or healing perspective.

By consciously visualizing a different, more supportive outcome, the brain can modify emotional responses and change the way memories are encoded. Just as external suggestions can distort memory, therapeutic visualization can rewire the brain's emotional associations with past events, making the experience of healing profoundly transformative.

The IFS "do over" exercise involves picking a traumatic time in the past and deciding to visualize reliving it but altering the event to prevent the trauma and gain strength. After reading about this technique, I decided it made sense to start at the beginning. I reflected as far back as I could while deeply meditating and trying to remember the earliest times I felt traumatized. There were many occasions to reflect on, several of which I had never even thought of as being horribly bad. I came to understand it's common to minimize the mental distress associated with past traumas. This, I learned, is a common avoidance and coping strategy, especially when the trauma was caused by a caregiver that you relied on for safety and survival.

One of my first traumatic memories was something I'd occasionally bring up with friends to laugh about. I was probably just approaching my third birthday. It's one of my earliest memories. But I can still clearly recall my father snatching away my baby blanket in dramatic fashion and taking it out back of the house to dispose of it for good. I was attached to the blanket. I called for it when I was tired or wanted a nap, and I slept with it every night. When I started teething, I chewed on the edge of it. I've read that babies who aren't breastfed often bond with items like blankets. Joking aside, the connection I shared with that blanket at that time was powerful. It was literally my security blanket.

In my meditative state, I could clearly recall the exact feeling I had when my father, a large powerful man, the head of the household, the person who was supposed to protect me, stormed out to the backyard in anger that morning so long ago. What followed was unthinkable to me: He tossed it onto the backyard barbecue grill, poured lighter fluid on it, and sparked it up. I looked on, horrified.

Going back to that memory as an adult, I empathize with my childhood self. I see myself as a toddler in a yellow flannel onesie, my tiny hands pressed against the single pane of the storm glass door, looking out at the concrete slab patio, the barbecue high in flames, and my blanket, turning to char. The sun was filtering through the lilac trees, and I felt the warmth on my face. It's funny how many details you can recall from the memories with strong emotional attachments. That sunshine was enhanced by the flames of the burning blanket.

I'll never forget the feeling of loss that happened in that moment. I sobbed. My eyes filled up with so many tears, I couldn't see clearly. My breath was out of control; as my chest heaved so heavily, I recall that it alone was alarming to me. I had no ability to understand what was happening to me. It was like an out-of-body experience. A profound sense of loss and complete helplessness washed over me, and I believe some serious wiring modifications were ingrained in me that morning—a loss of innocence, and likely my first tragic exposure to what is said to be a great source of human mental struggle: the lack of permanence of things, when we realize nothing is permanent, including us.

My sense of security vanished from me that morning. My memory of that day ends there. As I detached from what had happened, my sobbing subsided, and my focus shifted. I can remember noticing how strange and pretty the colors of dancing fire and sunlight, red, yellow, and orange, blurred through my tears.

This memory stirred another of sitting on the kitchen floor surrounded by yelling and screaming. My father, drunk, angrily threw our dog, just a puppy, across the room. The kitchen table was upset, spilling cutlery to the floor. That memory ends the same way, with a flickering light reflecting from the forks and knives bouncing onto the tiled floor. As if in slow motion, the light patterns became my preferred focal point among the chaos.

I realize so many people have suffered trauma with orders of magnitude greater than mine, but I've read that it's common, in those moments, to escape mentally and emotionally from these situations with the same sort of out-of-body experience I felt. When triggered, some people feel numb in the parts of their body where they were abused. They often can't recall many of the details, and they may not remember who abused them or how. But they might remember a detail such as the wallpaper they stared at during the abuse. Later, they might be triggered by a normal encounter, sexual or otherwise, and experience numbness in parts of their body, and even remember clear images or details—the wallpaper, for example.

Prior to engaging in IFS exercises, I had never really considered these events or several others as being that big of a deal, and I never considered how they might have impacted my life. I had told myself that sure, my dad was a drinker, and sometimes he drank too much, and stuff happened. But he was just trying to toughen me up, right? He was preparing me for the world. "It's a jungle out there", he'd say, and "You need to be tough and never let anyone push you around". Sometimes he would lose his temper. But his bullying came from a place of love, I told myself, because he didn't want me to get hurt out there in the big, bad world. I held on tight to the idea that most of his treatment of me just made me stronger and the better for it.

No doubt I had been wired to be tough and never let anyone take advantage of me. My dad's tactics fired up that protective part of me, which stuck with me throughout my life. I tried to recall every detail of some of my "Adverse Childhood Experiences". I imagined how I had felt in those moments. The words that sprang to mind weren't, "Dad loves me and wants to protect me". No, the words and emotions that came to mind were "horror" and "petrified". Those were my true emotions, as a toddler, an adolescent, and a teenager. The man who was supposed to protect me often snapped and turned on me. I often felt helpless, unsafe, and exposed. Nothing could protect me from the world, and I could never be truly safe, not when my own father was so unpredictable and seemingly dangerous. No one could be trusted. No one could protect me, and I couldn't protect myself.

With this memory fresh in my mind, I moved on to the next step of the "redo" that instructed me to rewind traumatic scenes after attempting to visualize every detail of how I felt and how they actually happened. Then when replaying the scene, instead of being a helpless child, I was to view the entire scene as a third party, and as the adult I am now. I imagined traveling back in time and standing in the doorway of my childhood kitchen, knowing what was about to happen. To my left stood my drunken, twenty-six-year-old father, about to explode in anger, while on the floor sat my infant self, playing with a toy and unaware of what was about to happen. I visualized myself back in time, peering into the kitchen of my childhood home, and I focused on that little child with great sympathy. Feeling my own fatherly protective instincts activated, I felt pulled to reach out and help my child self. So small and vulnerable, and deserving of protection. I felt the same overwhelming desire to protect him that I felt as soon as my own children were born.

Next, I visualized turning my focus on my father. He didn't seem as big and scary as he was when I was small. He looked like a confused, angry young man who had drunk way too much. Surprisingly, I wasn't angry, and I wished I could help him too. Now a man in my fifties, he seemed like a young man in need of guidance rather than the father figure he was to me back then. Following the IFS exercise instructions, as if back in time, I walked over to this man, my father, and I said all the things that needed to be said. I just let it flow. I didn't yell at him. Instead, I forgave him. I embraced him and told him I understood he was an emotional mess—that I knew how he had suffered too. I told him that I hoped he was at peace and even wished, for him, a future redo of his own. I hold on to hope there is a multiverse, and a different life possible for his spirit, where he won't make the same mistakes.

I felt compassion and sorrow for his loss of all the years that have passed since he died so young. He never got to be a grandfather or do all the things he wanted to do. He didn't see his kids grow up and achieve various successes because, thanks to him, they were tough and resilient. I had forgiven him years earlier, but this was the first time I felt like I had expressed it to him, if only in my imagination, through this exercise. The effect on me was powerful and profound. Like I said, it was a true epiphany, and that's why I'm sharing it. It was like visiting with my father's spirit after all these years and telling him I was okay and that I wasn't angry.

I paused to breathe, reflect, and release some pent-up emotions, then continued following the IFS "do over" instructions. I connected with my infant self by visualizing picking him up and hugging him tightly, saying all the things that should have been said by a caregiver back then. The things that come naturally to me now as a father. In this memory redo, I prevent the trauma altogether. The goal is to comfort your former self, assuring "everything's going to be okay" and that "I won't let anyone hurt you". Imagining holding that toddler, his head resting softly on my shoulder, was a powerful and cathartic experience.

The final step in the exercise was also the most electrifying. The instructions directed me to place myself back in the body of my child self and replay this newly created redo version of events.

As this scene begins, I'm back on the kitchen floor and vulnerable once again. I once again imagine the scene is about to play out as it did so long ago. The fear starts to well up in me, and I feel the anticipation of terror, feelings of dread, helplessness, and fear because of what's about to follow. But instead of letting my old memories play out, I visualize trying to look at the doorway and see my adult self enter the scene. Amazingly, as soon as I visualize the adult version of me arriving on scene, all the fear-related feelings disappear, and I feel safe. Seeing my adult self triggered a feeling of complete confidence that everything was going to be okay because "I know this guy and he's surely going to protect me". The feeling was incredible. At that moment, I realized I had someone to depend on and trust, who could always look out for me and keep me safe. That person was me and I wanted to hold onto that feeling. I wanted to be able to trust myself to take proper care of myself for the first time in my life.

The experience of that first IFS exercise had me wanting to revisit all my past traumas and create redos to heal them. I also theorized in part why this exercise is so powerful. I think it's like how some people feel when they give themselves over to a higher power. They feel safer, as if there is always someone watching out for them and no matter what happens, there is some sort of plan. Anyhow, this experience was, for me, a major epiphany.

REVISITING THAT DAY

Following the traumatic experience of trying and failing to save someone from drowning in a submerged vehicle, when I first dove in the water, I found it very unsettling to not be able to see well. For over fifty years, I'd been fine swimming underwater in murky lakes, eyes open without a mask on. I grew up even enjoying swimming in thick seaweed beds looking for large fish and turtles. During late-night sauna and lake routines, I would swim long distances underwater and pop up to playfully startle my friends. As an adult, I took up scuba diving in lakes and oceans and would occasionally do underwater dock work with extremely low visibility. But here I was now, feeling anxious and imagining that I could see a car door faintly in the distance when I swam underwater. The fight-or-flight chemicals even surged in my body. There it was, front and center. No denying it. I had been traumatized, and I had to face the fact that I wasn't as mentally tough as I would have liked to imagine. I couldn't just brush off what had happened that day and go on with my life with ease. My instinct was that I had to get back on the horse. I had to force myself to get into the water, open my eyes, and keep doing that, until I felt comfortable again.

The following day after the drowning and trauma, I sat on my dock with a hangover, alone and questioning myself. What had triggered me to pour a couple of bottles of wine down my throat and chain-smoke a pack of cigarettes? I sat on the dock and took some deep breaths. I had to figure out this relationship I had developed between being upset and calming myself with alcohol. Where and when did this all start, anyway? What led me to using alcohol this way?

I was reminded of my teen years when I first started drinking. I guess I started making choices to indulge in comfort foods around the same time. Whenever I was sad, angry, or frustrated, I'd turn to food, drinks, sometimes recreational drugs, and occasionally cigarettes. Dealing with my problems this way didn't solve them, but it helped me avoid thinking about them, at least for a time. Those "solutions" quickly turned to habits that I didn't outgrow but carried into my professional life as an adult. At various times in my life, I got into the habit of having after-work drinks to relieve the stress of the day, just like my father used to do.

The financial sector has historically been well populated with high-functioning alcoholics, and I had become one of them. My coping strategies for managing stress weren't just suboptimal; they were having a negative impact on my health and my personal life. Back around 2010, instead of looking into the underlying causes, I just wanted to treat the symptoms. I wanted to figure out how to stop being so upset. I had to learn how to stop being angry.

This led me to a book called *The Art of Happiness* by the fourteenth Dalai Lama, Tenzin Gyatso, and psychiatrist Dr. Howard C. Cutler, which emphasized the self-destructive nature of anger and hatred.[3] I learned that being angry is like poisoning yourself to try to hurt your enemies—a powerful idea that came to me while reflecting on the teachings. Dealing with difficult people was always going to be necessary at work and in life in general.

Part of this process also involved identifying those people and events. Certain people in my workplace were bullies, and they were sometimes cruel to the staff. Even though they rarely jousted with me, whenever I saw it or heard about it, I would be triggered and want to step in, often with a very combative approach. Those times made me angry, but I eventually realized I could deal with people like that in a calm, reasonable way, without getting stressed out and upset. If I allowed myself to get worked up, my breathing grew shallow, and my

3   HH the Dalai Lama and Howard C. Cutler, *The Art of Happiness: A Handbook for Living* (Riverhead, 1998).

brain and body didn't get enough oxygen. I'm sure my blood pressure rose too. None of that was good for me. Recognizing it was the first step toward defeating it. Then I made a rule for myself: Even if I did get angry, I wouldn't drink.

I had to learn how to rewire myself for the better, not just for me, but to enable my family to respond to adversity in healthier ways without negative consequences. I sought to break the habit of soothing my nerves with booze or ice cream, while maintaining my passion to fight for my beliefs.

Sobriety is not free of being a traumatic trigger in and of itself. Meaning the fear of drinking again can be itself clutter on the subconscious stage and influence the efficiency of how you apply yourself. And I was concerned that I would have my first "sobriety-induced fear" after returning home from a health retreat.

My house was well stocked with beer, wine, and hard liquor, the typical stockpiles that suited my lifestyle. My homes had wine cellars, liquor cabinets, and even dedicated kitchen wine fridges, all loaded with my favourite wines. I'm not talking boxed wine here. I was going home to be once again surrounded by delicious high-quality bottles— reds, whites, and champagnes to enjoy with meals or a perfect one to match with any occasion.

I didn't know what I was going to do with all those bottles. I also didn't know how life would change with my friends. Many of my best fun-loving pals shared my passion for food and drink. Would I go back to that lifestyle, resume old habits? How would my friends respond to my wanting to go on a serious health journey? Back at home in Collingwood, I stood in front of my wine fridge, curious as to the kinds of emotions it might inspire.

I had completed several IFS exercises and wondered which "parts" of me would speak up. Would part of me say, "It's okay, you've earned this. Just have a glass tonight. It's not a big deal"? This wasn't the first time I'd taken a break from drinking.

Going for a dry January or February had been attempted many a year and sometimes I made it through an entire month. More often,

I'd get two or three weeks in, drop some pounds, start to feel really good, and rationalize that I'd reset my health enough.

This time, I had read so many books and listened to even more audiobooks. I wondered if things might be different. I didn't know if this knowledge, and what I learned, and the therapy exercises I'd done would be powerful enough to override the parts of me that wanted me to crack open a fine bottle of wine to pair with a delicious meal.

So, it was to my surprise that as I returned home and stood looking at my wine fridge, I heard a different voice than normal. Softly, but clearly, as if from over my left shoulder, my own fatherly voice whispered, "You don't need that. I got you and I'm never gonna let anyone hurt you". It was a voice from the part of me I had tapped into to soothe my infant self in my IFS redo exercises, repeating what I had said. I paused and reflected that I had achieved a new consensus. I would no longer let parts of me make choices that would hurt me.

I was really tapped into my internal dialogue and working hard to be as mindful as possible. I realized that the calm, soothing internal voice typically didn't get involved in my food and drink choices. There was usually a lot of autonomic consumption or when I was hungry, tired, and needing a break, it was entirely different parts of me saying, "It's cocktail hour". I was stunned by how quickly that simple exercise had changed my way of thinking.

The dormant self-care part of me was awakened and empowered, as if I had flipped a crucial epigenetic switch. I finally felt certain that I was no longer willing to accept my doing what parts of me knew I shouldn't be doing.

Another very positive aspect of IFS therapy is the lack of blaming or shaming. According to prominent therapists this is a key element. I had to acknowledge that the protective part of me wasn't trying to hurt me, but rather to protect me. These amazing exercises changed me. For the first time, I felt a different kind of confidence and knew the changes I was making were going to stick.

My experiences with IFS have been profound. To get healthy, I had to do what so many of us don't want to do, which was admit that I needed rewiring. I had to dig into my past and recall painful memories instead of avoiding them. I had to break autonomic habits while also recognizing my many dopamine-related addictions and decide that pursuing healthier life choices might just lead to a much happier life.

The path to making good choices that lead to better long-term decisions and help us achieve our three-pillar, mind, body, and financial goals requires tapping into our drives, hashing out our triggers, and learning to separate our emotions from rational decision-making.

This is how we can change our behaviour patterns. By repeating better behaviours, we can then reinforce the small wins, and we become hardwired to continue and even accelerate down the path we choose. This is highly preferable to a life where we are easily triggered and constantly fighting not to give into our most primitive biological drives.

This is related to Freud's theory that humans have a sort of primitive brain and a logical, socially conscious brain, and the idea of id, ego, and superego. The greatest obstacle between a person and their goals is the mental game. Educating yourself on these obstacles and planning to overcome them can help you reach your goals, but too often, we don't follow through. Repeated setbacks followed by emotionally painful self-shaming results in a programmed aversion to even trying to change. Often followed by adopting avoidance strategies that can involve adopting a belief that we don't want to change. That's why it's so difficult to succeed in change without first identifying what might be holding us back. Taking the time to reflect on what our bad habits do positively for us and then strategically replacing them with better choices that accomplish the same positive goals is the best path.

I often think this relates to the "shadow self" that Buddhists warn against developing. When I compared Eastern philosophies, Freudian theory, and IFS therapy, I found similarities. Blending is when the self gives up its role as independent arbiter and doesn't succeed in obtaining a consensus on our life's path from all our parts. Instead, it often lets one part lead alone. Typically, a protective part then blends with the self and takes over our actions in an unchecked, unaccountable fashion, regardless of the consequences. When we blend with a protective part, we might just engage in distracting behaviours that might show up as avoidance and neglect. In extreme cases, the blending can lead to life-threatening actions. A serious drug addict can give over control to a part, the shadow self, that decides it's best to just escape life's difficulties in a drug haze, believing it's protecting them from the mental anguish of a sober reality.

Blending is also seen in some high achievers who go all in on building a business or accumulating extremely high net worth. They have a financial goal or a ranking they believe will make them happy, but when we allow our egos to drive the bus, and no matter how big the business grows or how much money we make, it will never be enough.

Jim Carrey once said, "I think everybody should get rich and famous and do everything they ever dreamed of, so they can see that it's not the answer".

When you are focused on a singular goal for happiness, it's easy to lose focus on the many other important things in life that are critical to happiness. Devoting all our energy to professional and financial success, and comparing ourselves to the success of others, often comes at a cost to our physical and mental health, as well as our relationships. This corrupts the soul and leads many to compromise themselves with poor ethical decisions that create stress and often leads to a chain of negative outcomes.

CHAPTER 10

UPDATE THE WIRING

IF AN ACTIVITY CAUSES HIGH STRESS OR NEGATIVE EMOTIONS, you may be triggered to revert to other autonomic behaviours that may be good or bad for your health. Our wiring is often designed to avoid stress and negative emotions, especially as it applies to social situations. We don't want to be disliked or cast out from the herd, which was evolutionarily devastating to an individual's survival. People want to be part of a family. We cannot survive on our own. When things go wrong within our family and friend groups, among our colleagues and communities, we suffer a great deal of stress. So, we are firmly wired to avoid being cast from our various peer groups.

When I learned all this, I thought, "bingo"! That is what triggers my unhealthy coping strategies. This wiring likely goes back to my teenage years, when I had to deal with periods of elevated emotional stress, anger, and sadness by knocking back a few drinks or eating ice cream. I carried those coping strategies into adulthood, and when I suffered from high stress due to the pressures of corporate management and high volatility fund management.

When you're in a high-pressure decision-making capacity, you're not always the most popular guy in the room. There's a lot of conflict and many battles. Companies grow and people want to go in different directions. Tough choices make some happy but others angry. I was also dealing with the typical stressors of commuting to work and managing time for family life. Not prioritizing my health allowed me to become ground down. I didn't appreciate that stress and anxiety actually leads to thinning of our cells' plasma membrane decreasing our ability to filter our signals. This actually disrupts our ability to focus while making us more likely to make knee-jerk reactions in stressful social situations. When you hear someone say, "He's got thin skin, be careful what you say to him as he will take it to heart or you'll trigger him to rage", understand that this actually is a very intuitive statement that has a basis in biology.

I also became fascinated by how much my emotional wiring and autonomic behaviours were actually controlling my responses, actions, and behaviours. By studying epigenetics, I found that some of my wiring was bad or broken, but I also discovered some pretty good wiring that had clearly helped me in the past. I identified parallels between my good wiring and my successes, as well as my bad wiring and my troubles.

I was raised to be extremely skeptical of scams and too-good-to-be-true offers. To dig in, do my own homework, and make the effort to understand rather than memorize information. I was fortunate to be raised to take the shot, get back on the horse, and accept failures as temporary setbacks—to brush them off and take them in stride.

I've made plenty of investment blunders. I've also explored and abandoned many career paths along my journey. The key has been digging in, in times of adversity, and having the confidence that the path forward comes with hard work and continued learning, with realizing not to doubt myself because it didn't serve me. I was lucky to always instinctively believe that getting down to do serious work, along with deep focus, leads to a good place. But there is no sense in pushing yourself to excel at something you don't enjoy.

My broken wiring included a lack of discipline and concern for my long-term health. I was wired to put my body's short-term needs first and often make unhealthy choices that gave me quick relief from stress. My chief priority was family finances, just as my dad's had been. I was a provider, and my health took a back seat. Fortunately, I realized that a key part of being a provider for my family required fixing my bad wiring—including some of the wiring I had inherited and developed by patterning myself after my dad.

To demonstrate leadership to the people I loved, I had to rewire myself. A good provider is also a role model for the people they care about, especially their children. A major driver for taking on a brain rewiring challenge was acknowledging that, due to my repeated struggles with depression, I didn't really care about my longevity. Who wants to live forever when right now isn't that great? But understanding epigenetics and how I could pass on these traits to my kids scared me to death. I was hungry to dig in and do the mental work and heal myself, for me but more for my children.

Mindfulness may be an overused word, but we're moving on now to discuss thought patterns and strategies. It's time to explore our mind's wiring with respect to being present, and to being able to make reasoned, versus impulsive, choices. Making choices based on how we want to be wired versus how we are currently wired. Our cellular makeup and microbial influences in our guts are only a tiny fraction of what makes us human, distinguishing us from the rest of the animal kingdom. Most of our DNA overlaps with other organisms, including bacteria, mice (85 per cent), and sharks (60 to 70 per cent).

We can change and become the people we want to be. It's time to analyze our wiring and not accept the status quo and eliminate habits that don't serve us.

Understanding epigenetics is empowering. Just knowing it exists should encourage everyone to take charge and change their wiring.

My curiosity was raised with the realization that my behaviours might have been passed on to my children. This added passion and purpose to my desire to change. Ready for the next stage, I knew I would have to dig into my mental state and become mindful of what was going on not only in my gut and body but also in my head. I had to overcome the false narratives that held me back, and change my lifestyle, even though I knew that meant likely losing touch with friends whom I shared many unhealthy activities with. I wanted to change and see if I could roll back the clock to feel ten or even twenty years younger.

This is not a matter of willpower or mental strength or a result of weakness. It's my firm belief that too often people with metabolic dysfunction, due to unhealthy mitochondria, experience sudden low energy availability with hypoglycemic shock symptoms. Recognizing this is crucial because the narrative in society around unhealthy people often points to a lack of willpower, laziness, or weakness. But it's the very cells in our bodies that stop us in our tracks when we run short of physical and mental energy.

No amount of mental willpower can stop this from happening. Fit people and even average healthy people cannot fully understand how hard it actually is at first for people with dysfunctional mitochondria and/or a weak liver to ramp up exercise at first. When one's health is seriously out of whack, we are just too poor at converting fat stores into energy. I urge people who have failed in the past to not give up but instead follow their deepest desires into this health journey because they really can change. It doesn't have to be so hard, and they will succeed if they take it slowly and remember to be kind and patient with themselves every day.

Rewiring is best achieved by replacing a bad habit with a good habit. If we only take away part of a habit that gives us neurochemicals we crave and don't replace it with a good substitute we end up with a void, as we find ourselves frustratingly low on some neurochemicals. In other words, it's best to replace our bad habits with good ones that provide the same neurochemicals, until they become autonomic. For example, let's say that on Tuesday evenings you have a habit of sitting in your favourite chair and watching Netflix with a glass of wine. If you remove only the glass of wine from that habit, you'll likely find yourself sitting, watching, and craving in an unsatisfied state, feeling like something is missing. Success comes when we swap out a nonperforming habit for a new habit that gives us the neurochemicals and endorphins we desire and then adding or "stacking" onto the new habit.

Here in Toronto, there is great swap-out story that has led to a tremendous business model. During COVID-19 a local finance guy—recently sober—wanted to create a social event that wasn't booze dependent. He started inviting neighbours over to hang out, talk, sauna, and cold plunge. It was a big success. Based on that he raised money and launched Othership, a socially minded sauna and plunge experience where the sauna is huge, DJs play, there is a light show, and talking is encouraged. It can be a lively experience akin to a classic "pregaming" event before going out except without the booze. Othership is coming to America, and it seems that people are hungry for positive swap outs. This strategy is far better than simply doing the same thing you used to do, while omitting the thing that actually gives you the dopamine hit. This is why "willpower" alone isn't the answer. But if you do start making small habit changes that are rewarding, and stack them, it will in turn grow your "willpower".

Habit stacking works by taking advantage of the brain's reward system and using it to build stronger, more persistent behaviours over time. When you stack a new habit onto an existing one, the brain forms a new neural connection by linking the new action to an already established routine. This process activates the brain's reward system, particularly the release of dopamine, which reinforces the behaviour and makes it feel rewarding. As the brain starts to associate the new habit with positive reinforcement, it becomes easier to repeat the action, leading to a more automatic response. Over time, this strengthens the neural pathways associated with the new habit, which in turn supports the development of mental tenacity.

As the brain becomes more accustomed to reinforcing small actions consistently, it grows better at sticking to challenges, boosting resilience and persistence. This is because the brain's reward system not only motivates the completion of a task but also improves the brain's ability to stay engaged with long-term goals, building the mental fortitude required to persevere even when faced with obstacles. This is why I am unconcerned where you start. Or how small the change is. The focus is permanent changes that are stackable. As you start swapping out nonperforming habits for ones that help you, they will in turn increase and rewire your reward systems which in turn makes new habit formation easier, which in turn grows the tenacity center of the brain—the anterior cingulate cortex (ACC). Again, why not take advantage of this positive feedback loop of change? And it is not just your brain that can be conscripted into this reward center-focused positive feedback loop. Have you heard of the hope molecule? Another biological wonder locked inside us.

When you exercise, your body generates positive endorphins, but there is so much more. Exercise forces muscles to secrete a compound often referred to as the "hope molecule", primarily linked to the release of dopamine. When we engage in physical activity, our muscles experience stress and microtears, which trigger the release of signaling molecules that not only help muscles recover and grow stronger but also stimulate the brain's reward centers. This surge of dopamine leads to an immediate boost in mood, motivation, and a sense of well-being, which is crucial for creating a powerful positive feedback loop in the brain.

As dopamine levels rise, they act as a natural antidepressant, often more effective than prescription medications in some cases. This is because dopamine doesn't just enhance mood—it also strengthens our sense of hope, fueling a belief in our ability to achieve goals. Over time, this rewires the brain, fortifying neural pathways tied to reward and reinforcing behaviours that lead to success.

The effects of this brain rewiring extend beyond physical and mental well-being—they can influence areas like financial success as well. When dopamine boosts motivation and focus, it increases productivity and goal-setting abilities, making it easier to take decisive actions that improve your financial situation. This might involve pursuing career opportunities, making smarter investments, or simply cultivating a mindset of abundance and possibility.

As financial stability improves, the cycle of hope and motivation strengthens even further, creating a compounding effect that amplifies both your financial and emotional well-being. The more success you experience, the more dopamine is released, further reinforcing positive behaviours and thoughts.

In this way, exercise not only reshapes your body and mind but also creates a dynamic feedback loop that improves all aspects of your life, including your financial health. The hope molecule turns exercise into a catalyst for growth, helping to build a resilient mindset that drives continuous success in both personal and financial realms. With use—and thanks to neuroplasticity—regions of the brain can grow, and new wiring is added. Put aside negative self-talk and remove any self-doubts or limitations. Be open to reshaping your mind and body to achieve the success you desire and become wired for success. Another element I want to talk about conscripting into your "co-vitality spiral" to supercharge your life—take advantage of your transgenerational epigenetic inheritance.

Transgenerational epigenetic inheritance refers to the process by which epigenetic changes—such as DNA methylation or histone modifications—are passed down from one generation to the next, influencing gene expression without altering the underlying DNA sequence.

This all sounds really complicated. Think of DNA as a massive instruction manual to build and operate all our intricate inner workings. Over time, we can make notes on these instructions, such as to ignore parts of the instructions or to utilize them now. We can basically operate histones like dimmer switches. There are intensity levels around what the instructions tell cells to do, so those switches might be off, on, or at different levels of intensity. We can also write new instructions that affect our bodies' responses to stimuli.

We have repressors, which can turn genes all the way off, and we also have silencers. Histones can wrap tightly around a gene, making it hard to access and express. There are also things called transcription factors and enhancers that can increase the rate at which genes are expressed. There are many unknowns about how all these things really work and all the factors that go into causing different mutations and our ability to repair our DNA with stem cells, both naturally and possibly through stem cell therapy in the future.

For example, people have different fight-or-flight instincts depending on how they're wired, which impacts our decision-making process. Think about how this affects our response to fire, which everyone fears to a degree. If you've been around an intense fire, you know the sight and the smell, and you've heard the loud crackling.

Depending on your history with fire, being around one may spark a painful emotion. You may be triggered to back away further and more quickly than other people. If you're from a family of firefighters, you may be comfortable staying closer to a fire than most people, while remaining calm. If you, your parents, or your grandparents experienced a tragedy that involved fire, you could be wired to be much more cautious around flames and even have a fire phobia.

Most animals are wired to be afraid of snakes. A rustling sound in a bed of leaves makes us jump, or it makes our heartbeat faster. The sound of a hissing snake or the sight of a poisonous snake, with its unique color pattern, triggers us. Our bodies are wired to jump away from these sorts of threats. Interestingly, when we are triggered, our bodies might stay at an elevated response level for hours. So just a little rustling after the initial experience will elicit a more heightened response than it did the first time, because we're sensitized to it. In modern life, a tough day with office arguments can send us home with a short fuse and low tolerance for adversity.

Our bodies are wired to quickly flee from various threats, and this response extends to human interaction. We can be attracted to certain types of people on a sort of "vibe level". We also pick up cues instinctively that some people aren't to be trusted. This is a learned sense, but it's also passed on through epigenetics. So, we are born with some while others are nurtured. There's a cultural aspect, and we have a strong and well-developed hunter-gatherer herd mentality. These reactions vary by culture and even influence investment outcomes as they affect crowd psychology, the formation of bull market blow-offs, bear market bottoms, or even cause stock market crashes.

The four parts of epigenetic wiring include, first, sensory input and neural activation. Second, signal processing occurs in the synaptic strengthening in the brain. Third, there is biochemical signaling, and fourth is gene expression. These steps result in epigenetic modification. Modification includes memory consolidation and storage, which is the process of becoming epigenetically wired through our life experiences. The more intense an experience, the stronger the brain and body become wired to perform or react in the future.

These changes can occur in response to environmental factors like diet, stress, and lifestyle choices, and can affect the health, behaviour, and even financial decision-making patterns of future generations. To consciously tap into this inheritance and create a positive feedback loop between health, mind, and finance, you can begin by adopting lifestyle habits that foster physical well-being, mental clarity, and financial acumen. Regular exercise, proper nutrition, and stress-reduction practices like meditation or deep breathing not only improve your immediate health but also influence the expression of genes related to resilience, cognitive function, and emotional regulation.

As your physical health improves, your mental state follows, boosting your motivation and ability to make wise decisions—whether in managing your finances or setting new personal goals. These positive mental and physical shifts trigger a cycle of success: Improved health leads to clearer thinking and better financial choices, which in turn reinforce your well-being.

Moreover, the epigenetic changes you create through these actions may influence your children and even grandchildren, shaping their genetic predisposition toward health, productivity, and prosperity. By consciously choosing habits that promote health and well-being, you are not only enhancing your own life but also contributing to a generational legacy of positive epigenetic inheritance that can elevate both your children's personal and financial growth.

Getting the body and mind wired with good autonomic habits is central to achieving the three pillars of mental, physical, and financial excellence. We can accomplish this thanks to neuroplasticity, which is our ability to grow and rewire regions of the brain. This happens when we challenge the brain to work hard, demanding more and better wiring. Practice makes perfect, and repetition is a major contributor to rewiring. Once our brain recognizes that we're going to be calling on it to do the same thing repeatedly, it responds by hardwiring the task. The process known as "chunking" is when the brain learns to perform a sequence of actions in an autonomic fashion, freeing up higher-level brain capacity to be free to focus on additional, perhaps more important, tasks or learning. This also helps the brain conserve energy.

Historically, it was useful for times like picking fruit while also needing to be on the lookout for approaching lions. Or in modern times, washing the dishes and watching a hockey game. Which activity do you want to be autonomic, and which would you rather focus on?

There's a lot of debate about multitasking because when you are doing two or more complicated things at once, your cognitive brain is actually switching back and forth between activities so quickly, you are not aware of the effect of shifting thoughts. The critics of multitasking argue that you end up doing both tasks with subpar performance. But there's no doubt that there are significant benefits to the practice of accomplishing basic tasks while engaged in higher-thinking cognitive work. I've consumed countless audiobooks while getting exercise climbing hills and believe the pairing of such tasks can make both more enjoyable and productive.

Once autonomic, repetitive tasks are directed by the brain's basal ganglia, a group of structures that play a pivotal role in habit formation. As we repeat behaviours, deep in the lower center of the brain, the basal ganglia learn to take over control of operations from the prefrontal cortex. This frees up capacity in the prefrontal cortex, the top layer, executive-function part of the brain where we have our higher levels of intelligence, memory management, and emotional regulation. Through determined effort to wire the basil ganglia to perform increasingly complicated tasks, they can take on more and more tasks while freeing the inner executive to pursue greater challenges.

Chemical messaging, or messenger reinforcement, occurs as well to hardwire autonomic habits. This is the production of neurochemicals that reward the brain for success with learning. I'll talk about this more when we get into the flow state, but it's worth mentioning here because it's a key to hardwiring new habits and right-sizing challenges that result in success and producing happiness and positive reinforcement. If the brain enjoys an experience, it wires it, so when we do it again, our focus is on making incremental improvements.

If a task or challenge is too easy, it's boring, so our brain doesn't bother to wire it. We lose interest. If the task is too difficult, we become discouraged, and the ego seeks to forget it. Without dopamine or other pleasant chemicals to make us feel good, we simply don't desire to repeat the activity. If a task is too stressful and ramps up cortisol production, we can become wired to have an aversion to the activity.

Parents sometimes encourage this positive wiring by allowing their kids to win at a game that's just above their skill level. The positive chemicals that reward them make them feel good about their progress and they are encouraged to repeat the activity and improve. If the child fails miserably at a task, they can become wired to avoid ever doing that task again.

CAN'T I JUST TAKE A PILL?

Why can't I just take a synthetic version of something positive like the hope molecule? Recently, I read an article about the discovery of a new molecule humans produce when we exercise that acts as an appetite suppressant. The journalist's article immediately focused on how soon this molecule would be synthesized. My immediate thought was, "Why not just accept this as a benefit of exercising instead"? If the body gets these hope molecules in a pill, will it eventually lose the ability to produce its own? If it stops producing that molecule, are there repercussions, like, does it also stop making other molecules our bodies need? Maybe the synthesized version isn't as good as the natural one and doesn't deliver all the benefits, so we are then shortchanging ourselves in the short term and possibly forfeiting our ability to create the superior molecules in the long term. And then what happens if the person stops taking these pills?

A significant part of the pharmaceutical industry is in the business of trying to identify molecules in the human body and then synthesizing them. This is the core of drug discovery and development. The first step is to identify a molecule and its potential significance—its role and what it does for the body. As more molecules are identified and baseline levels in healthy people are established, scientists work to discover patterns and anomalies.

For example, say someone has an illness and their doctor runs a battery of tests on them and discovers they have too much of one molecule and not enough of another. Perhaps the molecules the person is lacking can be supplemented with a synthesized version, e.g., a drug. Studies are then undertaken to see how a patient responds to the drug and, if proven effective and safe enough, the drug is approved.

But more and more scientists and doctors are speaking out against this entire process because it can simply mask a symptom instead of dealing with the underlying problem. For example, dealing with inflammation causes short-term relief, but it doesn't address the cause of the inflammation. So, the patient thinks they're being treated, but other symptoms arise as a result of the untreated underlying problem. It's becoming clear that the pharma and entire medical industry is far too focused on developing drugs with recurring revenue rather than looking for natural cures that are often related to diet, exercise, and lifestyle.

It's simply mind-blowing that the human body is capable of synthesizing more than a trillion different types of molecules. Our bodies often develop and produce new ones in direct reaction to threats to our immune systems.

The pharma industry has barely scratched the surface of understanding the human body's vast intricacies. Scientists have identified and synthesized only a small percentage of the key molecules produced regularly. Reports, studies, and opinions vary on the subject, but the consensus is the average body produces over ten thousand unique molecules for everyday living, and scientists only have a good understanding of between 30 and 50 per cent of them. We also often only have a very limited understanding of the many different roles a molecule might perform.

Thinking about this, the adage "use it or lose it" haunts me. What happens when we substitute a natural molecule for a synthetic one? Does it affect things in the body we're not aware of and set off chain reactions? For example, scientists have recently suggested that people with Parkinson's disease should delay taking dopamine medication for as long as possible because although it gives short-term relief, statistics now show that it might actually speed up the patient's deterioration.

The best pharmaceutical genius in the world is actually built into our bodies. We can create over a trillion different molecules. Drugs have a place in treating people and bringing relief, but maybe they shouldn't be the first solution. I believe a vast movement is underway to fully understand how to maximize our mitochondrial health. Mitochondrial health results in upstream cellular health and function, and this means healthy organs, glands, and bones. The roles mitochondria play are practically endless. It has a hand in just about every biological function, illness, and disease, not only in humans, but in every plant and animal as well.

We've touched on many key functions of the mitochondria, but I can't stress enough how these amazing little organelles have their hands in everything. They're at the core of all cellular functions, and they might play a major role in fixing nearly anything that's out of order in any cell in our body. Once I understood all this, I wanted to do everything I could to maximize the number of mitochondria per cell in my body and optimize their health. I wanted to leverage this knowledge to become as healthy as possible. I saw this as a clear-cut, amazing investment—a no-brainer if you will, because targeting mitochondrial health is good for the entire body, including the brain.

Olympic athletes are believed to have the highest number of mitochondria per cell among people due to the regular activity demands on their bodies. Endurance sports also demand prolonged, intense power, which leads to increasing mitochondria numbers. Conversely, sedentary people tend to have fewer mitochondria per cell. Mitochondria are always on the move. They change shape as they perform different functions, and take on very different appearances, depending on the type of cells they're in. Mitochondria increase their numbers by engaging in fission and splitting into two. They reduce their numbers in a fusion process where two mitochondria fuse together and become one. They also recycle themselves to improve efficiency and the health of the overall mitochondria population of a cell.

Duplication, or fission, happens when a cell has trouble meeting the demands put on it by the body, especially when a cell is worked hard so that all the ATP is used up and the mitochondria are then signaled to increase their numbers.

Consider all the functions of the mitochondria and the spin-off effects of having increased numbers of mitochondria, such as the likely benefits on immune function and body functions. Given the molecule-producing abilities of the mitochondria, and the supporting role that plays with other organelles in the body, and the cellular health benefits of building and maintaining healthy mitochondria, it seems intuitive that the more mitochondria, the better.

PART THREE

DEPLOY

Biology-Based Change

CHAPTER 11

TRAINING AND TRUSTING YOUR SYSTEMS

A GOOD FRIEND OF MINE IS A TV DIRECTOR AND FOR ONE OF his shows he spent a weekend with a Navy SEAL Team Six which was described to him as the team that—the leader could "neither confirm nor deny"—was the team that executed Osama bin Laden.

The leader of the team and my friend hit it off—even though they came from very different worlds—and over a beer the Team Six leader got into the Navy SEAL mental game.

Death doesn't care about your motivation.

The Navy SEALs are big believers in ability-based execution. Obviously, they train extensively physically and in weapons skill, but what caught my interest is how they train their brains. But first a little explanation of the Navy SEAL hand-to-hand combat fighting style. As it was described to my friend the Navy SEALs employ a style they called "compressing time". They literally bet their lives that their skill set is better than their enemies' skill set and so they try to create the most stressful, inhospitable, chaotic environment possible which takes the luxury of time away from the enemy. So, when they enter a combat situation they go as quickly as they can. Creating as much chaos as they can. As overwhelmingly as they can.

When you think about it, it makes sense. For the highly skilled, what appears to be a marginally more difficult environment can seem absolutely impossible to a less skilled person. For example, if Stephen Curry had to bet his life on a three-pointer competition why wouldn't he want to make the environment that he competes in as stressful and inhospitable as possible? The harder the challenge the more it tilts the field in the more skilled person's favour. It lowers the chance of a "lucky streak" and takes away most of the advantage "motivation" provides.

So, the Navy SEALs drill constantly. Train constantly. And to fully leverage their physical and skill base training, they train their brains to take away doubt. Take away distraction. And they do it in as many different chaotic and stressful environments they can think of. They call it stress inoculation. And for the inoculated, their skills can be translated to action in the most undiluted way. And the most ideal mental state the Navy SEALs train to keep their fighters in is "the zone", otherwise known as the flow state.

"Stop trying to hit me and hit me".

—MORPHEUS, *THE MATRIX*

Flow state is that exhilarating, effortless moment when you are fully immersed in an activity, where time seems to disappear, and every action feels instinctive and aligned. In flow, you're not consciously thinking about what you're doing—your mind and body are in perfect sync, allowing you to perform at your highest level without self-doubt or distraction. Whether you're working, creating, or engaging in sports, flow occurs when the challenge you're facing matches your skill level, and you're so deeply focused that the task itself becomes its own reward. It's that sweet spot where concentration is razor-sharp, and the energy you put out feels like it's flowing through you, rather than from you. When you tap into flow, you unlock your full potential and experience a profound sense of satisfaction and accomplishment.

To understand flow—the state of total absorption and effortless excellence—we must venture deep into the brain. Imagine a symphony of neural activity, each section playing its role with perfect timing. This is flow, a physiological marvel where measurable changes in the brain reveal why it feels so transcendent and why it makes us so effective.

Flow begins in the prefrontal cortex, the part of the brain responsible for executive functions like planning, decision-making, and self-regulation. As we engage in a challenging but manageable task, a fascinating process called *transient hypofrontality* takes place. This isn't just poetic imagery; it's measurable in a laboratory. Functional MRI (fMRI) scans reveal a decrease in activity in the dorsolateral prefrontal cortex during flow. This "quieting" of the brain's command center helps silence the nagging inner critic and frees us from distractions like self-doubt or worrying about the past and future.

At the same time, a cascade of neurochemical changes transforms our mental landscape. Scientists measure elevated levels of dopamine, a neurotransmitter linked to motivation and reward. Dopamine doesn't just make us feel good; it sharpens our focus, enhances pattern recognition, and primes us for sustained effort. Blood samples taken during flow also show increased concentrations of norepinephrine, which heightens alertness and speeds up reaction times. This is the brain on high alert, yet paradoxically calm—laser-focused but free of stress.

Then come the brain waves. Using EEG (electroencephalogram) technology, researchers observe a shift toward theta and alpha waves, which dominate during states of relaxed focus. These brain wave patterns are slower than the high-frequency beta waves of everyday problem-solving but faster than the delta waves of deep sleep. Theta and alpha waves reflect a state where the mind is both relaxed and alert, an ideal balance for creativity and insight. At peak moments of flow, bursts of gamma waves, the fastest of all brain waves, ripple across the cortex. These waves are the markers of high-level cognitive processing—moments of clarity when disparate ideas coalesce into solutions seemingly out of nowhere.

Perhaps the most remarkable aspect of flow is its neurochemical cocktail. In addition to dopamine and norepinephrine, the brain releases endorphins, natural opioids that reduce pain and create feelings of euphoria, and anandamide, a lesser-known molecule aptly nicknamed "the bliss molecule". Anandamide enhances mood and lateral thinking, allowing for creative leaps and connections that are elusive in ordinary consciousness.

Flow doesn't just feel good—it's a state of optimal performance that can be objectively measured. Scientists can observe increased connectivity between the default mode network (DMN) and the task-positive network (TPN)—areas of the brain that are usually at odds. During flow, these networks synchronize, a phenomenon known as network integration, allowing the brain to function more holistically. This harmony is fleeting; it dissolves when the task is completed, but its effects linger.

The process doesn't just end with the momentary high. Longitudinal studies using advanced imaging techniques like diffusion tensor imaging (DTI) show that repeated experiences of flow strengthen neural pathways. The more time we spend in flow, the more robust these pathways become, particularly in areas related to focus, problem-solving, and emotional regulation. It's as if the brain learns to make flow easier to access the more often it happens.

To the scientist, flow is a dance of chemistry and electricity, of deactivation and synchronization. To the individual, it feels like magic. But there is no mystery in its mechanisms, only awe at what the brain can do when everything aligns. Flow, it seems, is not just an experience—it's a demonstration of the brain operating at its full potential.

CHAPTER 12

RELAXED READINESS, THE GATEWAY TO FLOW

HAVE YOU EVER SEEN A CAT POISED TO LEAP? ITS MUSCLES ARE loose, its eyes focused, and its body completely still—until the perfect moment. Then, without hesitation, it springs into action with precision and power. This is the essence of relaxed readiness: a state of calm, yet alert anticipation. When cultivated, it becomes a powerful catalyst for entering and sustaining the elusive flow state.

Flow requires focus, engagement, and alignment of skills and challenges. But getting there is not about straining every muscle or forcing your mind to comply. Instead, it's about creating the conditions where readiness meets ease. Flow cannot be willed; it has to be invited.

THE ESSENCE OF RELAXED READINESS

Relaxed readiness is the balance between tension and tranquility. It's not idleness, nor is it hypervigilance. Instead, it's a state of being fully prepared for action without the burden of stress. Think of a martial artist standing in their fighting stance—not stiff, but steady; not passive, but patient.

This state is crucial for flow because:

- *It Lowers Resistance*: Tension creates mental and physical blocks, while relaxation removes them.
- *It Sharpens Focus*: A calm mind expands awareness, allowing you to absorb the full spectrum of information before precisely directing your attention where it matters most.
- *It Enhances Agility*: Flexibility, both mental and physical, allows you to adapt quickly to challenges, a hallmark of flow.

WHY TENSION KILLS FLOW

Many people mistakenly believe that effort alone leads to flow. They push harder, overthink every action, and try to brute-force their way into the zone. This approach is counterproductive because:

- Tension narrows your focus, making you less aware of subtle cues.
- Stress floods your body with cortisol, reducing creativity and impairing decision-making.
- Hyper-fixation on outcomes disconnects you from the process, a key component of flow.

Flow thrives not on force but on finesse. Relaxed readiness is how you set the stage for that finesse to emerge.

Considering that our consciousness is illuminated by brain cells that can also be preoccupied with subconscious thoughts, it is clearly best to cultivate a consciousness that utilizes as much of our brain cells as possible when trying to understand a new environment, problem, or task.

Relaxed readiness in this context means that the cognitive system is in a prepared but not overly engaged state, where attention is available to focus on relevant information but hasn't yet been activated to its fullest extent. This concept could be expressed in several ways:

BACKGROUND ACTIVATION

In a state of relaxed readiness, the brain is primed and ready for new information, but it is not yet actively focusing on any specific stimulus. In its relaxed state the mind is cleared of any high-priority tasks. It's a kind of open waiting state with quiet confidence but prepared to consider and perform when called on. Like casually glancing through magazines in a waiting room before a meeting you're confidently prepared for.

LIGHTING UP FOR ACTION

When we are called out of the waiting room, our cells ignite with energy and eagerness and our complete focus is directed toward whatever information or stimulus demands attention—this is the content that is currently in the foreground of awareness. Relaxed readiness means that while attention isn't yet drawn to anything specific, the brain is ready to rapidly engage with information as soon as it is needed.

For example, in a low-stress situation, your mind might be in a "relaxed readiness" state, where you're open to perceiving stimuli or making decisions, but nothing urgent is demanding your conscious attention. Our focus is shifted quickly to a new stimulus, such as a loud noise or an unexpected event, when the need arises.

SUBTLE, BACKGROUND MONITORING

During relaxed readiness, the brain may also be in a state of monitoring multiple sources of information in the background without consciously focusing on any of them. Our relaxed state allows us to quickly transition to full consciousness with heighted awareness when something important or relevant requires attention. This dynamic can be compared to a pilot being in a relaxed readiness state while flying— actively scanning instruments and surroundings, but not focused on any one detail until a change or anomaly draws attention.

MINIMAL CONSCIOUS LOAD

In a relaxed readiness state, our mind is not overloaded with the need to process high amounts of conscious information. Our attention is not fully focused on any specific element of the environment, allowing for low mental energy consumption and leaving resources available for future shifts in attention. This helps the brain conserve resources and avoid cognitive overload, allowing it to spring into action when necessary.

PRIMED FOR ACTION BUT NOT OVERLOADED

Imagine a professional athlete before a game—there's a readiness in the body and mind to act, but no immediate need for intense focus. Multiple possible scenarios are available in a subtle, lightly activated state, so the athlete can quickly focus on any of them when the right cue rises from the pattern recognition success of our subconscious. Conversely, if the brain is currently burdened by unnecessary cognitive noise it will be unable to direct conscious attention where it's needed. We simply won't be able to see and seize opportunities because our consciousness is preoccupied with what we might feel is high-priority work. Opportunities that require focus to fully appreciate will never obtain the priority status to capture our attention.

To understand relaxed readiness scientifically, we must explore what is happening in the brain. EEG studies show that this state is dominated by alpha brain waves, oscillating between 8 and 12 Hz. Alpha waves are most prominent when the mind is calm yet attentive, like the mental state of a practiced meditator or an elite athlete before competition. This isn't a state of drowsiness; rather, alpha waves reflect a brain that is disengaged from overthinking but primed for responsiveness.

Layered beneath the alpha activity are low beta waves, often called the "active concentration" waves, operating in the 12–20 Hz range. These waves ensure that relaxed readiness isn't simply passive relaxation. Instead, they act as a neural "guardrail", keeping the brain tethered to the present moment and prepared to shift into high gear if needed.

Neuroimaging studies add further nuance. Functional MRI scans reveal balanced activity between the default mode network (DMN) and the salience network (SN). The DMN, responsible for introspection and daydreaming, remains quiet, preventing the distractions of rumination. Meanwhile, the SN, which acts as a spotlight for relevant stimuli, stays moderately active, scanning the environment for cues without overloading the brain with irrelevant data. This balance is crucial—it allows the brain to remain aware without being overstimulated.

On the chemical level, relaxed readiness involves a subtle interplay of neurotransmitters. There's a mild elevation of dopamine, fostering motivation, and serotonin, promoting calmness and emotional stability. Unlike the surges seen in flow, these neurotransmitter levels are steady, maintaining a sense of equilibrium. Blood tests and neurochemical assays often show a slight uptick in acetylcholine, a molecule associated with focused attention and memory consolidation. This chemical mix primes the brain for sustained alertness without the jitteriness of stress.

From a physiological perspective, relaxed readiness is a Goldilocks zone for stress hormones like cortisol and adrenaline. Studies measuring cortisol in saliva reveal levels that are neither too high (indicating stress) nor too low (indicating lethargy). Similarly, heart rate variability (HRV), a measure of the balance between the sympathetic and parasympathetic nervous systems, is typically high in this state. A high HRV indicates that the body can switch effortlessly between relaxation and action—a hallmark of resilience.

Perhaps most tellingly, relaxed readiness is a state of high interoceptive awareness. Using advanced neuroimaging tools like resting-state fMRI, scientists observe heightened activity in the anterior insula, a brain region linked to monitoring internal bodily states. This heightened awareness allows the individual to sense subtle changes—like a quickened heartbeat or a shift in breathing—without becoming overwhelmed.

Relaxed readiness is not about doing but about being ready to do. To the observer, it might look like stillness, but to the scientist, the brain is a hive of potential energy. The networks of the mind are synchronized, the neurotransmitters balanced, and the body perfectly calibrated to respond when the moment demands. It's a state of quiet confidence—a readiness that doesn't push but simply waits, knowing it will act when the time is right.

TRAINING THE MIND

Relaxed readiness is not a passive state but a dynamic balance of calm and alertness. It is the mind's ability to wait in stillness, prepared to spring into action when needed, like a coiled spring holding its energy in perfect tension. This state has long been prized by elite performers, from athletes to artists, but perhaps no group has honed it more rigorously than the Navy SEALs. For them, relaxed readiness isn't just a skill; it's a necessity for survival. Their training provides a powerful template for cultivating this poised state of mind.

The starting point for relaxed readiness is breath. The Seals practice a method called box breathing (breath in for four seconds, hold for four seconds, exhale for four seconds, hold for four seconds) and it helps transition out of a stressful experience. Neuroimaging studies show that relaxed readiness is characterized by dominant alpha brain. waves, oscillating between 8 and 12 Hz. Alpha waves are associated with a calm, open awareness, the same mental frequency observed in experienced meditators. But SEALs do not simply rely on calm; their readiness requires the sustained engagement of low beta waves, which maintain active focus. This blend of alpha and beta waves creates a mental state that is both alert and unburdened, where thoughts flow freely, but attention remains grounded in the present moment.

A critical component of relaxed readiness is interoceptive awareness—the ability to tune into the body's internal signals without becoming overwhelmed by them. The SEALs train for this through controlled exposure to high-pressure scenarios, such as "drownproofing" drills. In these exercises, trainees are bound by their hands and feet and tasked with surviving in water for extended periods. The goal isn't merely endurance but teaching the mind to stay calm and attuned to physical sensations under duress. Heart rate variability (HRV) monitoring during these exercises often shows a remarkable ability to maintain high HRV, a marker of resilience and adaptability.

The chemical landscape of relaxed readiness is equally fascinating. Blood work from SEALs during these practices reveals a moderate elevation in dopamine, which fuels motivation and focus, and serotonin, which promotes calm. This balance contrasts with the surging cortisol typical of untrained stress responses. Their bodies become adept at releasing just enough adrenaline to stay sharp without tipping into the exhaustion or tunnel vision that excessive stress can cause.

For civilians, training for relaxed readiness doesn't require a military regimen but does benefit from adopting these principles. Breath control, for instance, is accessible to anyone. The act of slowing and deepening the breath not only calms the nervous system but also cultivates a sense of agency over internal states. Similarly, mindful exposure to stress—whether through cold showers, timed challenges, or public speaking—can teach the mind to remain steady under pressure.

Ultimately, relaxed readiness is a skill that can be learned, practiced, and refined. By controlling the breath, tuning into the body, and preparing the mind, anyone can access this state of calm alertness. It is not a place of passivity but of power, where the mind is free of noise, the body is primed, and the moment is all that matters. As the SEALs demonstrate, relaxed readiness is not merely a mental state but a way of approaching life's challenges with poise, clarity, and unwavering focus.

A RELAXED READINESS PRIMER

1. *Start with the Body*: Relaxed readiness begins in your physical state. Use these techniques to prepare:

   A. Breath Work: Deep, diaphragmatic breathing signals your nervous system to shift into calm alertness.

   B. Dynamic Warm-Ups: Gentle stretches or movements awaken your body without overexertion.

   C. Posture Awareness: Keep a posture that feels strong yet natural, avoiding rigidity or slouching.

2. *Prime the Mind*: Your mental state is equally important. Here's how to set it:

   A. Mindful Presence: Spend a few moments grounding yourself in the present. Focus on your senses or use a brief meditation.

   B. Positive Intention: Replace pressure with curiosity. Instead of saying, "I must do this perfectly", think, "Let's see where this takes me".

   C. Visualization: Picture yourself moving through the task effortlessly, focusing on the process, not the result.

3. *Focus on Entry Points*: Instead of jumping straight into complex tasks, ease into them. Find a simple, engaging way to start—like warming up with scales before playing a full composition or sketching rough ideas before tackling a detailed drawing. This creates momentum without overwhelming you.

RELAXED READINESS AND FLOW IN HARMONY

Relaxed readiness is like standing at the edge of a diving board: poised, calm, and prepared to leap when the moment feels right. In this state:

- *You're Present*: Your mind isn't distracted by worries or consumed with future outcomes.
- *You're Open*: You're receptive to opportunities and challenges as they arise.

- *You're Fluid*: You respond to the demands of the moment with ease, not resistance.

When relaxed readiness meets flow, magic happens. Your movements become intuitive, your decisions effortless, and your performance extraordinary.

HOW TO MAKE IT A HABIT

1. *Practice Often*: Integrate moments of relaxed readiness into your daily life. Whether it's a pause before speaking, a breath before typing, or a stretch before exercising, these small rituals train your body and mind to enter this state more easily.
2. *Embrace Imperfection*: Let go of the need for perfection. Flow doesn't demand flawlessness—it requires presence.
3. *Find Your Balance*: Notice when you're too tense or too lax and adjust. Relaxed readiness is a dynamic state, not a fixed one.

THE REWARD: FREEDOM IN ACTION

Relaxed readiness isn't just a precursor to flow—it's a skill in its own right. Mastering it will make you calmer under pressure, sharper in your focus, and more fluid in your actions. It's the foundation on which flow is built, and the doorway through which you'll step into your greatest potential.

So, the next time you approach a challenge, don't rush in with clenched fists or a racing mind. Pause. Breathe. Find your balance. Then, move forward with ease, knowing that flow is waiting on the other side.

CHAPTER 13

RIDING THE URANIUM BULL MARKET WITH RELAXED READINESS

MARKETS HAVE A RHYTHM, AN ALMOST BIOLOGICAL PULSE THAT mirrors our own internal states. When you've been trading long enough, you develop what some might call a sixth sense—but it's really just heightened pattern recognition combined with a state of relaxed readiness.

That's exactly where I found myself in early 2020, watching the uranium sector with the same calm intensity I had back in my Sprott days. The first uranium bull market had taught me everything I needed to know. Back then, I'd learned to read the sector's vital signs—supply constraints, demand catalysts, and most importantly, market sentiment.

That experience wasn't just about making money; it was about developing an intuitive understanding of market cycles that would serve me well in the future.

Fast-forward to spring 2020. While others saw chaos, I recognized familiar patterns emerging. The uranium sector was being thrown away—again. But, in my remote woodland home, I was relaxed and ready. No anxiety, no fear of the plunging market, just clearheaded observation and patience. The market was showing me exactly what I needed to see.

The signals were there: artificial intelligence's explosive growth promising unprecedented power demands in the near future, electric vehicles ramping up, and global energy security concerns intensifying. But what really caught my attention was how COVID-19 was forcing uranium mines to shut down worldwide. This wasn't just another market disruption—it was the catalyst I'd been waiting for, albeit earlier than expected.

I'd originally anticipated waiting another year or so, expecting a final bankruptcy rinse-out in the sector. But sometimes the market presents opportunities ahead of schedule. The pandemic had unexpectedly accelerated everything, highlighting supply chain vulnerabilities and the critical importance of energy independence. Nuclear power, with its reliable baseload generation, was suddenly looking indispensable again.

The beauty of being in this state of relaxed readiness was that when the opportunity presented itself, there was no hesitation. The decision-making process was almost effortless—my first go-round with the sector from the early 2000s had trained my mind to know exactly what to do and I was drawn in with a rekindled desire for the predict, execute, and profit endorphin rush. I'd seen this movie before, and I knew how it would end.

This wasn't luck or timing—it was preparation meeting opportunity. The years spent understanding the uranium market's first bull run had created deep neural pathways, allowing me to recognize patterns that others might miss. When I saw the sector collapsing to such low valuations in the face of production shutdowns, and the shifting global energy narrative, it all clicked into place.

The investment approach was systematic and calm. No rushing, no second-guessing. Just methodical position-building in select uranium companies, knowing that the sector's fundamentals were stronger than ever. The world needed to double its electricity output to handle the coming wave of EVs and computing power. Nuclear wasn't just an option anymore—it was becoming the only viable solution for reliable, carbon-free baseload power.

What made this second uranium bull market different was my state of mind. During the first run, I was learning, adapting, sometimes reacting. This time, I was in flow—that perfect state where experience meets opportunity. The market was speaking, and I was simply listening and responding.

The results came quickly—within a year, some positions had increased tenfold. But the real victory wasn't in the returns; it was in the validation of a process refined over decades. It proved that when you combine deep market knowledge with a state of relaxed readiness, you can capitalize on opportunities that others might miss or fear to take.

As Seneca said, "Luck is what happens when preparation meets opportunity".

This wasn't just about trading uranium stocks—it was about the power of maintaining composure while others panic, about trusting patterns that you've seen before, and about being prepared to act decisively when the moment calls for it. In the end, the second uranium bull market wasn't just profitable—it was a master class in the art of relaxed execution.

CHAPTER 14

RIGHT SIZING THE CHALLENGE

For the Navy SEALs, achieving flow is not about chasing a fleeting high but about reliably entering a state of optimal performance under extreme conditions. Their methods, honed through years of experience and rigorous testing, offer a powerful roadmap for training yourself to enter the flow state.

Flow begins with clarity of purpose. The SEALs train to break down overwhelming tasks into manageable steps, each with a clear objective. This mirrors the first requirement for flow: a clear goal. When the mind knows exactly what it's aiming for, it can fully engage.

For SEALs, this might mean focusing solely on reaching a waypoint during a grueling mission rather than being consumed by the enormity of the task ahead. For civilians, this principle can be applied by defining specific, actionable goals for any task—whether it's writing an article, completing a workout, or solving a complex problem.

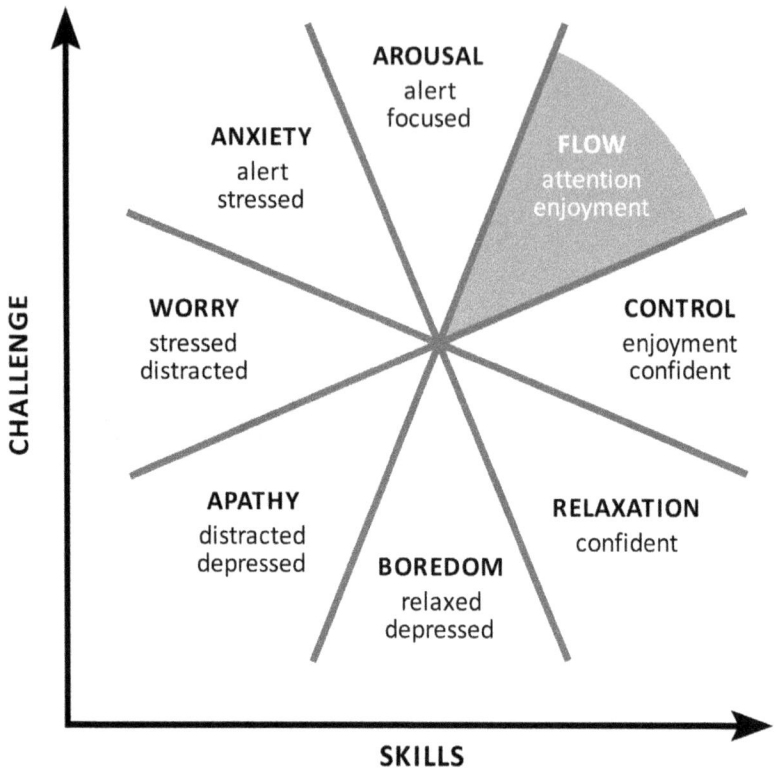

A diagram with vertical axis labeled CHALLENGE and horizontal axis labeled SKILLS, showing eight emotional states arranged around a center point:

AROUSAL — alert focused

ANXIETY — alert stressed

FLOW — attention enjoyment

WORRY — stressed distracted

CONTROL — enjoyment confident

APATHY — distracted depressed

BOREDOM — relaxed depressed

RELAXATION — confident

To achieve flow, the challenge must match your skill level. If the task is too easy, boredom sets in; too hard, and frustration takes over. SEAL training embodies this balance. Trainees are often pushed just beyond their comfort zones in exercises like simulated combat drills or the infamous "Hell Week". These challenges are intense but designed to feel achievable with focus and determination. This delicate balance stimulates the release of dopamine, a neurotransmitter that fuels motivation and sharpens attention. SEAL instructors create environments where small victories, like completing a drill or solving a tactical puzzle, provide immediate feedback, reinforcing the sense of progress critical to flow.

A vital part of SEAL training is learning to silence the inner critic and stay locked into the present moment. Neuroimaging studies show that during flow, activity in the dorsolateral prefrontal cortex decreases, a phenomenon known as transient hypofrontality. This allows the brain to bypass self-doubt and analysis paralysis, freeing up mental resources for creativity and focus. Through their training, SEALs learn to enter this state instinctively, even in life-or-death scenarios.

SEAL training also teaches the importance of deliberate recovery. Flow is an energy-intensive state that cannot be sustained indefinitely. By alternating between high-intensity drills and recovery periods, SEALs optimize their ability to re-enter flow when needed. For civilians, this might mean structuring your day to include intervals of deep work followed by periods of rest or lighter tasks. Recovery helps replenish the neurotransmitters like dopamine and norepinephrine that fuel flow, ensuring you can return to peak performance.

Finally, SEALs cultivate a mindset that embraces failure as part of the process. During training, mistakes are inevitable—and intentional. Instructors often introduce variables designed to make trainees fail, forcing them to adapt and remain engaged. This builds resilience and helps trainees avoid the frustration that can block flow. Adopting this perspective in your own life means seeing setbacks as opportunities for growth rather than as reasons to disengage.

Flow is not a mysterious gift reserved for the elite; it is a state that can be trained and accessed by anyone willing to practice the principles of focus, balance, and recovery. Whether through breaking tasks into manageable goals, controlling your breathing, visualizing success, or learning to embrace challenges, you can cultivate the conditions for flow. The SEALs show us that with discipline and intention, even the most extreme environments can become fertile ground for this extraordinary state of being.

THE FLOW STATE: LIVING IN THE ZONE

Buddhists meditate to reach a state they call nirvana, which is like being in the zone. A kind of "flow state" where you feel energy flowing in and around you. Endorphins and other neurochemicals are activated during this state. Activating these pleasing endorphins is necessary to create new wiring and cement epigenetic programming changes. While this benefits your mental state, it can also help improve your physical state.

You might be familiar with the song "Life in the Fast Lane" by the Eagles. It's about partying, but there are better ways to "lose your mind". The wild rock and roll lifestyles are no longer celebrated, as we've come to understand they burnt out or killed many of the superstars of earlier eras.

In fact, after watching countless documentaries on this life history of great bands it's clear nearly everyone that survived sobered up and completely changed their lifestyle. Playing music in a band is an incredible high, flush with many neurochemicals, and even generates a brain wave synchronicity of band members when performing in the zone.

Achieving this flow state can give you a high better than any drugs, quieting the cognitive part of your brain and bringing the present into full focus. Being in the zone or flow state is the only time the human body produces nearly all its wonderful neurochemicals at the same time. Depending on the activity you pursue to get into a flow state, you can produce neurochemicals such as serotonin, which is associated with happiness; norepinephrine, a chemical that plays a key role in focus, concentration, and alertness; and anandamide, which is referred to as the "bliss molecule", with anti-anxiety and antidepressant effects that can increase creativity.

Endorphins are natural painkillers, responsible for the "runner's high" that allows long-distance runners to run through pain. Our bodies also produce nitric oxide, which plays a supportive role regulating our neurotransmitters. There's also oxytocin, the "bonding hormone" or "love drug" associated with social bonding, trust, and relationship building. Engaging in a challenging group activity can enhance feelings of trust among the group, leading to elevated levels of oxytocin. During situations involving risk or serious physical challenges, your adrenal glands release adrenaline, which increases your heart rate, blood pressure, energy supplies, and a fight-or-flight response. People can become addicted to this feeling—the so-called "adrenaline junkie".

Imagine being in the flow state during a challenging, physically demanding group activity, especially one that includes an element of fear. Your body produces a lot of different chemicals, including cortisol, which reduces inflammation and contributes to wakefulness. Excessive amounts of cortisol can be negative, but the right amount keeps your alertness at an optimal level for the activity. Phenylethylamine is an organic compound related to amphetamines and found in chocolate. It's also produced naturally within our bodies, acting as a neuromodulator or neurotransmitter in the brain and is associated with excitement and elevated thrills, adding to overall intensity and pleasure. Gamma-aminobutyric acid (GABA) is the main inhibitory neurotransmitter, which occurs in the gut. When you are in the flow state, it helps modulate and control your anxiety, allowing you to remain calm and focused.

Acetylcholine is a neurotransmitter that's key for learning and memory, helping us lock in new skills. While in the flow state, we can consume and commit knowledge to memory at our maximum rate because we are supremely focused in a heightened dopaminergic state that triggers epigenetic programming and memory storage.

Glutamate stimulates excitement and learning and is balanced with GABA to keep us relaxed and not overstressed.

Releasing corticotrophin hormones helps us manage stress when we're in heightened states of awareness, such as while taking part in intense sports.

After learning about the flow state and thinking back to some of the best times of my life, I made a goal of seeking out flow state experiences as much as possible. You can encourage your body to produce the necessary neurochemicals to help you get there through meditation and other activities. When I'm doing something that's important to me, I try to get into that flow state right away.

Consider how even elderly people light up when you get them talking about times when they were in the flow state. Just recalling the memories of major achievements like intense sport wins from our youth gets those flow state juices flowing again. People are often able to remember every detail of some significant event in their past when they were really in the zone. They recall the euphoria they felt, and when it was over, maybe they collapsed, or maybe they cried tears of joy. It's a great feeling—the best rush ever. That's the power of the flow state, flush with all its neurochemicals. When you take part in activities like mountaineering, rock climbing, or other demanding sports, especially those that involve contact with other people, and where there's a bit of risk involved—maybe you could be injured or die—the flow state can be unbelievably intense. When you reach the top of the mountain or achieve some massive win, you get a massive endorphin release, and the memory of the event is strongly encoded to last a lifetime. It's a huge team-bonding experience and one of those feelings that must be felt to be fully appreciated.

We all can routinely find ways to achieve this feeling in our lives. The gateway is often said to be through the passionate pursuit of our curiosities with a motivating purpose.

Aristotle argued that "Happiness is the meaning and the purpose of life, the whole aim and end of human existence" without the scientific understanding of all the neurochemicals we produce in this pursuit. He argued that real happiness doesn't come from giving in to hedonistic pursuits or overindulgence in unhealthy habits that merely trigger primitive dopamine reward circuits. He believed in "eudaimonia" which was the ultimate purpose of life that results from pursing your highest good and living to serve your virtues. Following our curiosity in pursuit of challenging projects with a purpose that we are passionate about serves our virtues and when we do it well, we enter the flow state.

Again, you cannot "will" yourself into a flow state. Consciously willing yourself into a flow state is challenging because flow, by nature, happens when you're so immersed in an activity that self-consciousness fades. However, while you can't force flow, you can create the conditions for it to emerge. It's like planting seeds—you can't make them grow instantly, but you can prepare the soil, water them, and provide sunlight to increase the likelihood of growth. And— besides training relaxed readiness—you create the conditions of flow by practicing perfectly.

CHAPTER 15

PERFECT PRACTICE

PERFECT PRACTICE GIVES YOU THE EXPERIENCE WHICH BRIDGES relaxed readiness and the flow state. If you have grooved the necessary synaptic pathways and done the "dress rehearsal" for cell synchronicity, through practice you will have the skill set necessary to effectively utilize the flow state.

It's not about rote repetition but intentionality. While perfect practice can feel laborious at times, it lays the groundwork for flow. The precision you build through this disciplined approach becomes the muscle memory and mental clarity that flow thrives on. The relationship between flow and perfect practice is like that of a river and its banks. Perfect practice carves out the structure, and flow is the water rushing through. Without solid banks, the river meanders aimlessly. Without the water, the banks are just dry earth. So how do we break down the elements of perfect practice?

SLOW IS SMOOTH, SMOOTH IS FAST

The saying "Slow is smooth and smooth is fast" emphasizes the importance of controlled precision over hurried action when engaging in practice. By focusing on smoothness and eliminating mistakes, you can achieve greater speed and efficiency in the long term. It's about mastering the basics slowly and intentionally so that when the pressure is on, your actions become fast, fluid, and effective.

PRECISION OVER SPEED

The principle underscores the idea that focusing on getting the action right is more important than rushing through it. In tactical situations, hasty decisions or rushed movements can lead to mistakes like misfires, missing critical information, or creating unsafe situations. Precision and control allow for greater predictability and reliability. Learn it right, then get fast.

MASTERY THROUGH REPETITION

SEALs and other elite units practice their techniques over and over until they become second nature. Whether it's weapon handling, combat drills, or communication, repetition fosters smoothness. Once movements or decisions are smooth, they become faster because you can execute them without thinking about every individual step. Also known as grooving, the idea is repetition deepens the synaptic path between firing neurons making the task automatic.

NEVER FORGET INTENTIONALITY

When an individual or team "phones it in" even in practice, they might skip important steps, overlook details, or make poor judgments. Slow, controlled actions minimize errors, allowing the team to be more efficient in the long run. For example, if a team is rushing to clear a building and misses a door or an enemy, it creates unnecessary risk and delays. A smoother, more methodical approach ensures better outcomes. Again, practice perfect by executing perfect technique in more and more difficult situations and environments. And as they groove their smooth methodical approach they can go faster and faster perfectly.

The takeaway? It is much better use of your finite energy—surprise surprise—to invest in skill acquisition and mastery. Ironically the more you work on making action less conscious, the more effective your conscious becomes in being in ally in execution.

The Navy SEALs also focus a lot of the mental training on the speed they go from relaxed readiness to flow-based execution. The SEALs work on how quickly they can transition their attention and focus from wide and not intense, to narrow, intense, and hyper-focused.

When it comes to sweeping a room, let's say, the SEAL will go from trying to take in as much of the room as possible with their direct and peripheral vision until their wide vision highlights a threat or target and then they laser in.

THE SEAMLESS SHIFT: TRAINING THE TRANSITION FROM RELAXED READINESS TO FLOW

The transition from relaxed readiness to flow is the critical pivot where poised potential becomes focused execution. For the Navy SEALs, mastering this shift is the difference between staying ready and taking decisive action. Their training revolves around cultivating the mental agility and physiological control to glide from one state to the next, regardless of external chaos. This ability is not innate—it's trained. By examining their methods, we can uncover strategies to refine this transition in our own lives.

"There isn't tough. There is trained, and untrained".

—CREASY, MAN ON FIRE

1. PRIMING WITH INTENTION: THE ART OF PRE-ENGAGEMENT

I mentioned how important visualization is to SEALs. They are trained to focus their attention before engaging, aligning their mental state with the demands of the task. "Priming" is crucial in bridging the gap between readiness and immersion. Before a mission, operators spend time visualizing success, rehearsing scenarios with a focus on sensory details and emotional states. This primes the brain to recognize the flow-inducing moment when it arrives. Neuroimaging studies show that such visualization strengthens the connection between the salience network (which identifies important stimuli) and the task-positive network (which drives focused action).

In daily life, you can adopt this method by setting a clear intention before tackling a task. Take a moment to mentally rehearse what success will feel like, visualizing yourself fully engaged. For instance, before starting a complex project, imagine the rhythm of your work, the clarity of your thoughts, and the satisfaction of progress. This primes your brain to seamlessly engage when the moment demands.

2. TUNING FOCUS: THE TRIGGER OF TOTAL ATTENTION

In SEAL training, the moment of transition often comes with an external cue—a sudden command, a shift in terrain, or a change in the environment. The key is how the mind narrows focus without narrowing awareness. This process relies on a rapid increase in norepinephrine, a neurotransmitter that heightens alertness and reaction speed. SEALs train to respond to these cues with precision rather than panic, often through drills that simulate high-stakes decision-making under pressure.

You can train this in your own life by using small, manageable triggers to direct your attention. For example, before diving into work, you might create a ritual like adjusting your workspace or starting a specific playlist. Over time, these cues signal your brain that it's time to move from readiness into deep engagement.

3. ACTIVATING THROUGH SMALL WINS

Once the shift begins, the SEALs rely on momentum to lock into flow. The act of completing a simple, achievable task—like securing a piece of gear or clearing a small objective—triggers a dopamine release. This neurochemical surge rewards effort and primes the brain for sustained focus. Their training emphasizes breaking down large challenges into bite-sized steps, ensuring that each victory builds confidence and reinforces focus.

In your own practice, structure tasks to provide quick, tangible rewards early in the process. Starting with an easy win—organizing a workspace, writing a single sentence, or completing one push-up— can create the momentum needed to slip into flow.

4. LEARNING TO TRUST AUTOMATICITY

In flow, the brain shifts into a mode where decisions feel instinctive and actions unfold without conscious effort. SEALs train this automaticity through relentless repetition. By drilling core skills until they become second nature, they free up mental bandwidth for creativity and adaptability. This phenomenon is backed by research showing decreased activity in the dorsolateral prefrontal cortex during flow, allowing the brain's procedural memory systems to take over.

You can train this transition by practicing essential skills repeatedly until they feel effortless. If your goal is creative work, spend time mastering foundational techniques. If it's athletic performance, focus on ingraining key movements. The more automatic your skills become, the easier it will be to let go and let flow take over.

5. STRESS AS A CATALYST, NOT A BARRIER

SEALs learn to embrace stress as a gateway to flow. During training, they are placed in high-pressure scenarios designed to simulate the chaos of combat. These controlled environments push them just past their comfort zones while equipping them with tools like breath control and mental reframing to stay engaged.

In everyday life, you can mimic this by introducing moderate stressors that challenge you without overwhelming you. A tight deadline, a public performance, or a challenging workout can provide the right level of arousal to activate flow. The key is to maintain a mindset of curiosity and control, viewing stress as an ally rather than an enemy.

6. CLOSING THE LOOP: RECOVERY FOR REPEATABILITY

After intense drills, operators engage in deliberate decompression—breathing exercises, stretching, or simply reflecting on their performance. This recovery phase restores the brain's neurochemical balance, replenishing the dopamine and norepinephrine depleted during flow.

For you, building structured recovery into your day ensures that transitions from relaxed readiness to flow can be repeated without burnout. After a period of intense focus, step away for a walk, engage in deep breathing, or meditate. Recovery isn't just rest; it's preparation for the next round of flow.

The SEALs show us that the transition from relaxed readiness to flow is not about force but about alignment. It's about creating the conditions for the mind to shift seamlessly, like a wave gathering power before crashing into its peak. Through deliberate training, from breath control to visualization, from small wins to structured recovery, you can cultivate the ability to move into flow with ease. It is this ability—to shift from waiting to doing, from potential to performance—that transforms preparation into mastery.

THE OUTCOME: STRENGTHENING NEURAL PATHWAYS

When you exit flow, your brain isn't just "tired". It's stronger. During flow, repeated activation of neural pathways reinforces them through a process called *myelination*. This means that the skills you practice during flow become more automatic over time.

This is where the behavioural model comes in: The smallest amount of motivation paired with immense ability only needs a prompt to make flow more accessible. The more you engage this formula, the more you will access flow and you've not only completed the task in front of you but also set yourself up for greater success in the future.

FLOW AND FINANCE

- *Use flow to stay calm in high-pressure situations*: Volatile markets can trigger emotional reactions like fear or greed, which lead to impulsive decision-making. Entering a flow state helps you remain calm and focused during periods of market turbulence, allowing for more rational, data-driven decisions.
- *Flow helps manage emotions*: When you're in flow, you're deeply absorbed in the process, which helps separate emotions from investment decisions. This is particularly useful during major market swings, where being emotionally detached allows you to stick to your strategy without reacting to short-term noise.
- *Enhanced cognitive processing*: In a flow state, your brain processes information more efficiently, allowing you to recognize patterns and trends more easily. This can be especially useful in technical analysis, where identifying patterns like support and resistance levels, trends, or reversals in stock charts can lead to more profitable trades.
- *Sustained focus for deeper analysis*: Flow allows you to engage in deeper, uninterrupted analysis. By sustaining focus for longer periods, you can notice subtle trends or overlooked opportunities in the market, giving you a strategic edge over others who may not be as focused or thorough.
- *Quick, intuitive judgments*: Flow state enhances intuitive decision-making by allowing your mind to work quickly and efficiently. In fast-moving financial markets, being able to process large amounts of information rapidly and make intuitive judgments is crucial, especially for short-term traders or those in highly volatile environments.
- *Improving your reaction time*: Investors in flow can react more quickly to changes in market conditions. Whether you're making split-second decisions on stock trades or deciding to enter or exit a position based on new data, flow increases your responsiveness.

- *Deep learning through flow*: Flow states are excellent for building mastery because they allow you to focus on improving specific skills. In investing, this means consistently learning and refining your approach, whether it's understanding new financial instruments, exploring advanced trading techniques, or improving your analytical abilities.
- *Increased long-term learning*: Flow not only helps you perform well in the short term but also improves long-term learning. By spending more time in a state of deep focus, you absorb knowledge more effectively, allowing you to develop a more comprehensive understanding of the financial markets over time.
- *Flow promotes flexibility and adaptation*: Since flow requires a high level of engagement, it allows you to adapt quickly to new market conditions or unexpected changes. When you're in flow, you're better able to process new information and adjust your strategies without being overwhelmed by the emotional stress that often accompanies market changes.
- *Innovation and creative problem-solving*: Flow can lead to innovative thinking and creative solutions, especially in uncertain or complex market environments. By being fully immersed in the analysis, you may identify unique opportunities or alternative approaches that others may overlook.
- *Flow prevents burnout*: Investors often face mental fatigue and burnout from the constant pressure to perform. Flow helps mitigate this by making the work more enjoyable and immersive, reducing feelings of stress or exhaustion. When in flow, you lose track of time, and investing becomes less of a grind and more of a fulfilling challenge.
- *Sustaining long-term engagement*: Maintaining a sense of flow in your investment activities keeps you engaged over the long term. By continuously finding ways to enter flow, you can remain enthusiastic about market research and analysis, even in the face of challenges or setbacks.

MASTERY AND FLOW WITH INVESTING

The art of successful investing isn't just about spreadsheets and technical analysis—it's about developing an intuitive understanding of human behaviour and market psychology. Through diverse experiences spanning multiple industries, a distinctly different education background, and deep interactions with people across various cultures, I've developed a unique lens for spotting winning investments.

Think about how you instantly know which friends will love a new song on the radio. That same pattern recognition applies to stock stories. When you've internalized enough mental models of how different groups think and behave, you develop an almost visceral sense of which investments will resonate with the market. It's like feeling the pulse of collective human psychology.

The key is not waiting for perfect information before taking action. When you catch the first hints of a compelling narrative, it's often worth establishing a small position early. Just as you might share that perfect song with a friend before it hits the charts, you want to be positioned before the crowd catches on. Yes, thorough due diligence is crucial, but the magic happens when you can spot those early signals that others will soon see what you're seeing. This isn't just pattern matching—it's about developing a feel for the rhythm of the market through years of cross-disciplinary experience.

What separates great investors from good ones isn't just their analytical capability—it's their ability to synthesize diverse experiences into an intuitive framework for spotting opportunities. When you can feel the electricity of a great investment story in your bones, that's when you know you've reached that coveted flow state in investing.

TAKEAWAY FOR BEHAVIOURAL DESIGNERS

Flow is the result of precise triggers in the brain: a challenge that matches your skill, clear goals, immediate feedback, and an environment that minimizes distractions. Understanding and leveraging these mechanisms can help you design environments and habits that make flow a regular part of life.

When I look back at the parts of my life that I was at my lowest—depressed, dependent on booze, bad food, and distraction—I see it was also the times I least experienced flow. When I look back at the best times, I was in flow constantly. I was lucky that my transgenerational gift of "hunting big prey where people haven't looked" epigenetics easily jumped the tracks from big prey to big stocks allowing me to flow my way to financial freedom. But with the privilege of hindsight and the positive effect of visualization I can see that the pursuit flow state—regardless of task or starting position—might be the secret sauce here.

Curiosity, passion, and conviction create the groundwork for flow. The more you cultivate flow, the easier it is to invite it back. When you are completely lost, the important thing is forward motion. Any forward motion, regardless of what it is.

Maybe don't attempt to tackle the problem head-on. It might be a better energy utilization to tackle anything that makes you curious, passionate, and that you can tackle with conviction. And shelve "the problem" for now. Maybe you need to get better at getting better first.

Success is cross-trainable; success in any part of your life will make success in other parts of your life easier. That early success can start with just the way you talk to yourself. It can be as simple as a shift in attitude at first. Or focusing on your breath. What is important is applying right size challenges, automating them, and stacking them. Because the more you conscript your biology—regardless of what it is for—the more biology is working for you, not against you. Like I said at the beginning of the book, if you want to move a mountain, start with a single stone. It doesn't matter which stone you pick.

ADDED BONUS OF TRAINING YOUR MENTAL STATE

Science is now developing a much greater appreciation of the healing effects of the mind and the therapeutic benefits of being in different brain wave states. When we focus on external problem-solving we enter the beta wave brain state and its associated increased levels of stress-related neurochemicals like cortisol and adrenaline. They help us focus but if we maintain elevated levels for too much of our lives, these neurochemicals impact our healing ability and can lead to stress-related health issues. It makes perfect sense that when focused on external problem-solving, the body prioritizes energy for cognitive tasks rather than healing processes.

When we are relaxed and calm, we encourage our body to repair and rejuvenate with alpha waves. Stress-reducing neurochemicals such as serotonin give us a sense of well-being, supporting mental clarity and calmness. Theta waves occur when we enter deep relaxation, and they support mental and emotional healing. Delta waves occur during deep sleep and our body releases growth hormones and other essential molecules for tissue repair and immune system maintenance. Delta waves aren't just important; they are crucial for cellular repair and regeneration, as the body focuses on healing and restoring itself.

Likewise, when we actively focus inward, relax in meditation and mindfulness, and perform body scans, we can shift the brain into alpha and theta states, promoting the production of healing neurochemicals and proteins. This inward focus can enhance cellular communication and coordination, supporting the body's natural healing processes as it signals our cells to prioritize our healing.

In our most relaxed states, our body produces proteins, utilizes stem cells, repairs DNA, and generates new cells. When we consciously think about healing, our cells respond and engage in the healing process. When we are caught up in the drama of world news we too often get filled with stress and cause ourselves damage.

In essence, we must seek balance and create an environment that encourages alpha, theta, and delta brain wave activity to support the body's natural healing mechanisms, enhancing both physical and mental health. Prioritizing these states allows the body to focus on self-healing in a coordinated effort, maximizing its potential for recovery and well-being.

Many techniques are available for being more present. Breath work is an amazing practice for centering yourself (you must be tired of me saying this again, but really everything begins with the breath). It helps you acknowledge the effect of stress on your body and empowers you to let go of the anger or whatever is bothering you.

Progressive muscle relaxation is used in yoga and chakra therapy and in Buddhist meditation. It involves systematically tensing and releasing muscle groups to alleviate stress and create body awareness. I've practiced progressive muscle relaxation for years as part of my chakra exercises and found it very helpful.

Body scan meditation involves focusing on your body's sensations as you mentally "scan" regions of your body, which promotes relaxation and mindfulness. There's guided imagery, which involves visualizing peaceful scenes or positive outcomes.

At first, some people may find meditation difficult, boring, or even frustrating. Mindful walks that emphasize the present by noticing the sensations in your body and observing your surroundings are a good option. You can even stop and smell the flowers, as the old adage recommends. The goal is to be present and aware in nature, which is good for the brain.

With observation of thoughts, you take note of whatever thoughts surface when you're not trying to think about anything. Try not to judge your thoughts but rather be aware of emotional triggers associated with them and try to reduce their impact.

Gratitude journaling can also be a positive experience, uplifting your mood. This consists of writing down everything that you're grateful for and reminds you of what you have and may be overlooking or taking for granted.

Self-compassion exercises encourage you to treat yourself with kindness, understanding, and self-acceptance. Showing compassion toward others can also be a mood booster. Focused attention meditation involves concentrating on a single thing, such as your breath, a mantra, or an object. The idea is that focusing on just one thing calms your mind.

ADDED BONUS OF VISUALIZATION:
MANIFESTING THE FUTURE

Manifesting a positive future includes setting goals you want to achieve and identifying the steps to reach them. You can add visualization, where you picture yourself achieving those goals. Positive affirmations cultivate a positive mindset.

Challenging yourself to try new things can help with self-discovery and growth.

Also, read biographies, autobiographies, and memoirs of people you admire. They might inspire you to emulate them in some way.

Another way to manifest your future is to pick a time and a place in the future and imagine yourself there in great detail. When I did this exercise, I pictured myself at eighty years old, hiking to the top of a mountain in Arizona. It's warm and sunny out, but not too hot, and I feel great. In this vision, I'm happy and healthy, and so are my friends and family members who hiked up there with me. My grandkids would be there too, and they'd be proud of me for being able to keep up with them.

This creates new wiring similar to IFS therapy, but instead of a redo, it's a script for a future you want to manifest. You can imagine having a conversation with yourself or the other people in this vision and discuss what you need to do to create this future. Surprisingly, this exercise can provide clear direction on the steps required.

My visualization told me I would have to give up alcohol for a while and prioritize my health. I'd have to eat better, sleep better, and work on strengthening my back, legs, and cardiovascular system. Losing weight would also get me closer to that future.

I also imagined where that eighty-year-old man would be if he didn't do these things. I'd be on the couch eating, drinking, and watching TV. Maybe I'd be in a pine box. I sure wouldn't be on top of a mountain with my grandchildren.

The funny thing about this exercise is that I had been doing this sort of thing throughout my financial career, but I had never considered how much it shaped my future. Before choosing an investment,

I imagined how a company would evolve and how the market would play out. I would try to visualize how all the different types of investors with various investment styles would view a given company I was considering and how they would value it. But I also understood that by working hard and making smart investments, I would receive recognition and achieve my financial goals. I was confident that my dedication to hard work, learning, and understanding would result in a positive future.

Visualizing the future and plotting a course to become the person you want to be forces you to figure out what you must learn and do, so you can design a proper plan that works. You can't just expect to magically end up in success. You must research, develop, and implement the strategy for your journey to succeed, including doing the hard work.

Before I became president of a company, I had to picture myself running a company. I had to figure out which skills I needed and start acquiring them by reading books and talking to other people who knew more than I did about the role.

Detail your path as much as possible and be willing to revise it and continue to improve it. As you're building your plan, understand that not everything will be perfect or play out the way you expect. Expect to regroup and adapt as you hit setbacks or miss targets. Tweak your plan as needed. Monitor it and your progress and continue to grow as a person.

A commitment to constant improvement, resiliency, and researching and trying new therapies, then monitoring the results, along with a willingness to evolve with the changing world, strengthens your three pillars—mind, body, and financial health.

I believe top performers are epigenetically wired to generate positive neurochemicals when faced with challenges. Often, this starts with the simple visualization of a path to success. Modern science is starting to grasp the effectiveness of engaging in meditation and other exercises to create positive neurochemicals that assist with positive habit forming.

CHAPTER 16

BANKING ITERATION AND REAL-TIMING COURSE CORRECTION

LET'S KICK OFF THIS NEXT PORTION OF THE BOOK WITH A BIT of a summary of where we are. We started with the idea that time and energy are finite. That "life" (the expenditure of energy over time) does indeed end.

If we are sold on the idea that it is good to be goal oriented, then it would be logical that we would want to make sure that as much of our energy expenditure over time is in the service of whatever goals we have set.

Given Stanford Professor B. J. Fogg's model from *Tiny Habits* there is a better return on energy investing in abilities instead of motivation because—when prompted—high motivation/low ability is less reliable than high ability/low motivation.

We invest in abilities in many ways, but the most energy-efficient way is to break down our "goals" into smaller and smaller objectives that can be achievable and trigger a dopamine reward. Then we take these right size victories, automate them into habits, and stack them. The stacking and automating of these habits results in powerful change and better energy utilization.

Borrowing from the Navy SEALs we know that automating habits can be made more efficient by utilizing stress inoculation, "perfect" practice, relaxed readiness, and flow state.

We also know that increasing our efficiency of energy use in the service of our goals is helped by spending some time analyzing "energy leakages" like trauma, gut health, and the role of epigenetics in shaping our worldview.

Furthermore, training our consciousness helps us identify "blind spots", and improving how and what captures the focus of our attention can further improve our use of energy in the service of our goals.

I want to introduce another thought here, constant course correction. There was a study done on the difference between veteran and amateur blacksmiths with regard to their hammer swing accuracy. Obviously, the veteran blacksmiths were far more accurate in their strikes, but the reason why is informative.

The path the hammer swing takes for the amateur had less variability. Meaning they tried to repeat exactly the same path each time. With the immense amount of factors influencing the swing (muscle coordination, changes in environment, friction, air resistance), the more the blacksmith held on to the exact swing path, the less accurate the blacksmith was. The veteran blacksmith—utilizing a vast and automatic bank of swing "experiences"—was able to recognize subtle changes in swing mechanics and adjust the swing accordingly, creating a larger variety of swing paths but resulting in the strike being far more accurate than the amateur who had less variability. The takeaway here is the value of constant evaluation and course correction.

When it comes to "perfect practice" the stress here is on having intent to your practice, not the avoidance of mistakes. We want to make our practice as energy efficient as possible. And that is achieved by ramping up learning. Which requires—like the veteran black-smith—utilizing a vast and automatic bank of experiences. Failure and mistakes are a key learning portion of practice. Like the Navy SEALs, failure is part of "perfect" practice. We must have mastery through iteration. This ties into Malcolm Gladwell's concept of mastery—as outlined in his book *Outliers*—being ten thousand hours of perfect practice.

A veteran blacksmith's expertise comes not from avoiding mistakes but from recognizing and correcting them in real time. The blacksmith is focused on getting better at getting better. Similarly, progress toward your goals requires frequent adjustments based on feedback and changing circumstances. Every small adjustment improves accuracy and efficiency, much like correcting the hammer's swing. Life is dynamic, and external conditions often shift. Course correction ensures you remain flexible, adjusting to new challenges, opportunities, and insights. Goals themselves may evolve, requiring recalibration of your efforts to remain meaningful.

Constant evaluation isn't just limited to your performance, but you must be evaluating the value of your practice itself. This involves establishing feedback loops to monitor your progress. These loops help you identify what's working, what isn't, and where adjustments are needed. Internal feedback is where you reflect on your own performance, emotions, and results. External feedback is where you seek input from mentors, peers, or measurable outcomes (e.g., metrics, milestones). And like the multitude of course corrections in the veteran blacksmith's swing, each round of evaluation informs your next steps, creating a cycle of learning and growth. Like the blacksmith refining the arc of their hammer swing, your repeated small corrections compound into significant progress.

This habit also helps you with time management; small mistakes caught and corrected early prevent larger issues from derailing your progress. For example, recognizing poor time management early can save you from a missed deadline later. Regular adjustments keep you aligned with your goals, preventing stagnation or burnout. Correcting minor misalignments ensures consistent forward motion, even when progress feels slow.

Continuous evaluation deepens your understanding of your strengths, weaknesses, and tendencies. This self-awareness becomes a powerful tool for long-term personal and professional development. These can be daily, weekly, or monthly, depending on the goal. (Tools like journals, apps, or progress trackers can help.) We accept that plans may need to shift. Recognizing incremental progress reinforces motivation and keeps you engaged in the journey. It is important to remember at all times that progress is seldom a straight line. There will be plateaus, even reversals, but if you keep at it, the tenacity part of your brain grows allowing you to handle the inevitable ups and downs of progress.

This approach aligns with the growth mindset—the belief that abilities and intelligence can be developed through effort, learning, and persistence. Course correction embodies this mindset by emphasizing learning from mistakes and adapting, rather than striving for perfection early and giving up.

Having said all of this, we must also focus on the balance between patience and action: Course correction doesn't mean constantly changing your goals or strategies without giving them time to work. Patience is key for allowing actions to yield results. However, waiting too long to evaluate and adjust can lead to wasted effort. Finding the right balance ensures progress remains steady and intentional. Course correction is small changes within the framework of belief. You believe in a goal and are willing to learn from the mistakes along the way. No one is perfect out of the box; it is unrealistic to believe mastery is possible without some level of setback.

The secret to hitting your goals, much like the skill of a veteran blacksmith, lies in constant evaluation and course correction. Small, deliberate adjustments based on feedback and reflection ensure that you stay aligned with your objectives, adapt to changing circumstances, and refine your approach over time. Success is not about avoiding mistakes—it's about recognizing them, learning from them, and using them as stepping stones toward mastery.

CHAPTER 17

THE BALANCE POINT

WE HAVE SPENT TIME ON ANALYZING THE VARIOUS PARTS OF "you", how to recruit all of you into servicing the pursuit of your goals, and looked at how to "master mastery"—how we can get better at getting better. Old people tell young people all the time, real wealth is the freedom to use your time as you see fit. And for you to maximize your time under your control you must respect all three pillars—mind, body, and finance. Too much concentration in one leads to neglect in another. Without balance life can be good, long, or free, but not all three. So, what philosophical framework pairs well with this belief?

I want to explore the relevance of the Japanese principle of *ikigai*.

Ikigai (生き甲斐) is a Japanese concept that translates roughly to "a reason for being" or "a reason to live". It represents a sense of purpose or something that gives an individual motivation and satisfaction in life. In essence, it's about finding joy and meaning in daily living. While often associated with career and life goals in modern interpretations, its origins and applications in Japanese culture are far broader and deeply rooted in philosophy and tradition.

Ikigai is often visualized using a Venn diagram with four intersecting circles, though this specific representation is a modern Western adaptation and not traditionally Japanese. These circles are:

1. What you love (your passion).
2. What you are good at (your vocation).
3. What the world needs (your mission).
4. What you can be paid for (your profession).

The intersection of these elements symbolizes ikigai in the Westernized view, but in Japanese culture, ikigai can be much simpler (will get into that a little later). But first a history.

The term *ikigai* combines two words:

- Iki (生き): Life or being alive.
- Gai (甲斐): Value, worth, or benefit.

The concept can be traced back to the Heian period (794–1185), where early Japanese literature hinted at ideas resembling ikigai. At the time, *gai* was derived from the word *kai* (shell), as shells were considered valuable. Thus, ikigai implied something valuable that makes life worthwhile.

Ikigai has roots in Japanese philosophies influenced by Buddhism, Shintoism, and Confucianism.

Buddhism: Encourages mindfulness and finding joy in simple moments, which resonates with ikigai's emphasis on appreciating daily life.

Shintoism: The reverence for nature and the interconnectedness of life fostered a sense of purpose in communal and environmental harmony.

Confucianism: Promoted societal roles and responsibilities, encouraging people to derive meaning through contributing to the community.

After World War II, Japan underwent rapid modernization and societal transformation. The economic boom of the 1950s–1980s brought new interpretations of ikigai. With the rise of corporate culture, people began associating their sense of purpose with career and material success. However, this interpretation often led to overwork, challenging the balance between professional and personal fulfillment.

In recent decades, particularly with the aging population in Japan, ikigai has gained attention as a philosophy for longevity and happiness. Research on the Okinawan people, who have some of the highest life expectancies in the world, highlighted ikigai as a significant factor in their well-being. For Okinawans, ikigai often revolves around close social bonds, meaningful daily routines, and a sense of belonging.

Today, ikigai is celebrated as a universal concept that can help people balance their passions, responsibilities, and well-being. It has been adapted globally as a tool for self-reflection and personal growth.

While the Westernized interpretation often focuses on career alignment, the traditional Japanese perspective emphasizes small, intrinsic joys that create a fulfilling life. In essence, ikigai is not just about grand ambitions or lofty goals but also about cherishing the simple, meaningful moments that make life worth living.

Ikigai is not something explicitly "practiced" in Japan in a formal or conscious manner. Instead, it is more of an ingrained cultural philosophy that subtly influences daily life. Most Japanese people do not actively refer to the term or consciously apply a structured framework like the Westernized "four-circle" model. Instead, the concept is inherently woven into their way of living, shaping attitudes toward work, relationships, and personal fulfillment.

For many Japanese people, ikigai is found in the small, meaningful moments of everyday life rather than in grand achievements. Examples include:

- A parent finding joy in raising their children.
- A retiree tending to a garden.
- An artisan perfecting their craft.
- A community member participating in traditional festivals.

This reflects the traditional Japanese appreciation for *wabi-sabi* (beauty in imperfection) and *mono no aware* (awareness of the impermanence of things).

Japan's work culture has a complex relationship with ikigai. Many people derive a sense of purpose from their jobs due to the societal emphasis on contributing to the group (a concept rooted in Confucianism). However, the intense work ethic and long hours of Japan's corporate environment (often leading to *karōshi* or "death from overwork") can sometimes overshadow the positive aspects of ikigai. For some, their job itself is their ikigai, while for others, work is simply a means to support activities they truly value, like family or hobbies.

There has been a resurgence of interest in ikigai, partially due to its global popularity. Books, workshops, and seminars on ikigai are available, and some people consciously reflect on the term as part of their personal development. However, this level of self-conscious application is relatively rare compared to how ikigai is seamlessly integrated into traditional lifestyles.

Most Japanese people would understand the concept of ikigai but might not articulate their life purpose using this term. Instead, it naturally informs their values and choices. Older generations may find ikigai in familial roles or traditional crafts, while younger generations might explore it through hobbies, careers, or creative pursuits. In rural areas, where community ties and traditional lifestyles are stronger, ikigai often aligns with collective activities. In urban settings, individuals may find ikigai in personal passions or professional achievements.

Ikigai is a deeply embedded aspect of Japanese culture, even if it isn't explicitly "practiced" in a structured way. While people in Japan may not consciously strive for ikigai as a goal, the philosophy underpins their approaches to work, relationships, and daily life, emphasizing a quiet, enduring search for meaning and joy.

So why is the Venn diagram not the complete picture of ikigai? The relationship presented in the Venn diagram implies that we should constantly be seeking the "middle" of the diagram. That feels a little too restricted. Ikigai can flow between the elements depending on where you are at in life. Sometimes you do need to focus on compensation at the cost of the other elements. Conversely you may be in a better financial position and focus more on the non-compensation elements. Ikigai is a useful framework to evaluate the macros in your life. To adjust goals as life is constantly thrown at you. The importance of the philosophical process is to achieve feedback and evaluation without freaking out. Like the Navy SEALs practice stress inoculation to imbue the ability to monitor life and death without tripping into flight-or-fight adrenal response, you should be able to intellectually evaluate your goals and achievements without getting unduly emotional about it. In that way, it is useful to think of ikigai with the elements of purpose ebbing and flowing instead of being a strict balance.

Ikigai provides another plus as a philosophical framework. It gives great structure to your thoughts. Time for another quote:

"Be careful of your thoughts, for your thoughts become your words. Be careful of your words, for your words become your actions. Be careful of your actions, for your actions become your habits. Be careful of your habits, for your habits become your character. Be careful of your character, for your character becomes your destiny".

Be it attributed to Lao Tzu, Ralph Waldo Emerson, or Frank Outlaw, this quote is worth exploring what effect the intellectual framework of ikigai has on our thought process which in turn affects our mental and physical well-being.

Reconciling the principle of focused training with the Japanese concept of ikigai creates a holistic framework for discovering and aligning with your life goals. Training can strengthen coherence in decision-making by improving our conscious attention and integrating sensory, emotional, and cognitive inputs. It aligns well with the process of finding ikigai, as discovering your purpose requires deliberate, focused introspection and synthesis.

The relationship between ikigai and priority-based focus training lies in the way we emphasize focused attention and the allocation of mental resources to meaningful tasks. Ikigai is about identifying and focusing on what gives your life purpose, joy, and meaning. Ikigai helps you clarify what is most important to you (e.g., what you love, are good at, and find meaningful). Once you identify your ikigai, the brain naturally directs attention toward tasks and experiences that align with it. These activities are perceived as rewarding, making them more likely to occupy your conscious thoughts.

When you're pursuing your ikigai, you are more likely to enter a state of flow, where your consciousness is intensely focused on the task at hand. The relevance and intrinsic motivation provided by ikigai help sustain this focus, reducing distractions and enhancing productivity. Activities tied to it often evoke positive emotions, reinforcing their importance in your consciousness. Emotional significance plays a key role in maintaining focus. Tasks that align with your ikigai are emotionally salient, ensuring they "win out" in the competition for conscious attention.

With regards to "training your consciousness" you can fine-tune your attention by focusing on what aligns with your ikigai, and irrelevant or superficial concerns are filtered out. Conscious awareness of your focus influences choices, ensuring they are aligned with your long-term goals and passions. Think of it as the baseline evaluation tool of your course correction. Like the constant correction in the blacksmith's swing improves accuracy, repeatedly focusing on ikigai-related activities strengthens neural pathways, making these tasks feel more natural and effortless over time. Knowing your ikigai reduces cognitive overload by narrowing the range of activities you need to focus on.

When pursuing your ikigai, the brain is naturally more engaged, making it easier to maintain sustained attention. A clear sense of it minimizes internal conflicts over priorities, allowing our focus to remain steady on meaningful pursuits. Again, it shouldn't be hard and fast but used as a framework of course correction. The more you evaluate action within the framework of ikigai you will be able to automate course correction. Heightened consciousness enables awareness, epigenetics shapes adaptability, and mitochondrial health ensures sustainability—all essential for living in harmony with your ikigai.

The relationship between ikigai and the flow state lies in their shared emphasis on intrinsic fulfillment and the joy derived from meaningful engagement in activities. While they are distinct concepts, they overlap in key ways that help individuals lead purposeful, satisfying lives. Both ikigai and flow emphasize finding joy in the process, not just in achieving results.

Activities that contribute to your ikigai often put you in a state of flow because they align with what you love and are good at. Similarly, part of it involves doing what you are good at, which increases the likelihood of experiencing flow during these activities. Ikigai encourages appreciating the present moment, whether through small joys or purposeful work. Flow is essentially a state of deep presence and concentration, making it a natural extension of ikigai-driven activities.

While flow is more focused on the immediate experience, ikigai incorporates a broader sense of purpose and meaning. Engaging in flow-inducing activities that align with your passions and contribute to your sense of mission can deepen your ikigai. Both concepts reject overemphasis on external rewards (e.g., money, fame) and focus on sustainable inner satisfaction.

DIFFERENCES BETWEEN IKIGAI AND FLOW STATE

ASPECT	IKIGAI	FLOW STATE
Scope	A holistic life philosophy that spans all aspects of life.	A temporary mental state tied to specific activities.
Focus	Long-term purpose and meaning.	Immediate engagement and optimal experience.
Connection to Others	Can involve contributing to society or relationships.	Primarily individual and inwardly focused.
Temporal Nature	A continuous, overarching concept.	A transient state that comes and goes.

Ikigai helps you focus on activities that truly matter to you, which are often the ones most likely to induce flow. By pursuing your ikigai, you refine skills that help you take on challenges effectively, a key factor in entering flow. The sense of purpose from ikigai drives you to engage deeply in activities, setting the stage for flow experiences.

HOW TO COMBINE IKIGAI AND FLOW IN DAILY LIFE

- Identify Flow-Inducing Activities:
  - Reflect on tasks where you've experienced deep focus and enjoyment. Align these with your ikigai to make them a regular part of your life.
- Pursue Mastery:
  - Continually challenge yourself in activities tied to your ikigai. Growth in skill fosters more frequent flow states.
- Balance Challenge and Ability:
  - Ensure that the tasks you undertake are neither too easy nor too difficult to stay engaged and avoid frustration.
- Find Purpose in Small Moments:
  - Even mundane tasks can become flow-inducing if approached mindfully and aligned with your ikigai.
- Create a Flow-Friendly Environment:
  - Minimize distractions and cultivate focus when engaging in activities related to your ikigai.

Ikigai and flow are complementary: Ikigai provides a meaningful framework for life, while flow represents the optimal psychological state you can experience while engaging in activities aligned with your ikigai. Together, they create a powerful synergy that fosters long-term happiness, purpose, and peak performance.

Being mindful and thoughtful regarding one's own life's value aids in facilitating healing trauma and influences epigenetic re-switching, though the relationship is complex and operates through interconnected psychological and biological pathways. Healing from trauma involves addressing both the psychological and physiological impacts of adverse experiences. Ikigai, as a source of meaning and purpose, can play a significant role in this healing process. Remember when I said sometimes it could be better not to deal with blockage directly but to focus on things you can do or like to do? One of the by-products of meditating on ikigai is to rob trauma of its power.

Trauma often disrupts one's sense of purpose and connection.

Rebuilding a sense of ikigai helps individuals regain a framework for meaning, countering feelings of helplessness or disorientation. People who cultivate purpose after trauma are more likely to experience post-traumatic growth, characterized by increased resilience, personal strength, and appreciation for life.

Trauma often dysregulates the hypothalamic-pituitary-adrenal (HPA) axis, leading to chronic stress or hypervigilance. Fostering a sense of purpose by engaging in meaningful activities promotes mindfulness and emotional regulation, reducing cortisol levels and restoring balance to the stress response system. Social support is crucial for trauma recovery. Ikigai often involves a sense of mission or contribution to others, fostering deeper connections and support networks, which are protective against the effects of trauma.

Epigenetics refers to changes in gene expression that occur without altering the underlying DNA sequence, often influenced by environmental factors, behaviour, and emotions. Stress, trauma, and purpose all play roles in this dynamic system. Traumatic experiences can lead to epigenetic modifications, such as methylation of stress-related genes (e.g., the glucocorticoid receptor gene), which may perpetuate heightened stress sensitivity or emotional dysregulation.

As mentioned, these modifications can sometimes be passed on to offspring, creating intergenerational effects. Regular engagement in activities that give one's life a sense of meaning and purpose lowers stress levels, reducing the release of stress hormones like cortisol. This can reverse stress-induced epigenetic changes, restoring normal gene expression. Positive emotions associated with pursuing your ikigai—such as joy, fulfillment, and contentment—have been linked to beneficial epigenetic changes, including upregulation of genes related to immune function and downregulation of pro-inflammatory genes.

Activities that enhance ikigai, like mindfulness or meaningful social interaction, promote neuroplasticity (the brain's ability to rewire itself). This can influence epigenetic mechanisms, potentially reversing trauma-related changes. By promoting healing and resilience, ikigai could also impact the epigenetic profiles of future generations, reducing the transmission of trauma-related changes. It helps you pass on positive transgenerational inheritance breaking what some people call "generational curses".

Practically, focusing on life's purpose encourages mindfulness and living in the present, which has been shown to reduce trauma symptoms and improve overall well-being. Ikigai can help individuals reinterpret traumatic experiences as opportunities for growth or learning, which supports emotional resilience.

Biologically speaking, ikigai creates regulation in the HPA axis. HPA axis regulation refers to the balanced functioning of the hypothalamic-pituitary-adrenal (HPA) axis, which controls the body's stress response and helps maintain homeostasis by regulating hormones and various physiological processes. This system involves the hypothalamus signaling the pituitary gland to release adrenocorticotropic hormone (ACTH), which then prompts the adrenal glands to produce cortisol, the primary stress hormone. Proper regulation ensures that the body effectively responds to stress and returns to baseline afterward.

Dysregulation, caused by chronic stress or other factors, can lead to over activation or under activation of the HPA axis, resulting in issues like anxiety, depression, fatigue, or immune dysfunction. Restoring balance involves managing stress through practices like mindfulness, regular sleep, healthy eating, moderate exercise, and possibly therapeutic interventions such as adaptogens or cognitive behavioural therapy. A well-regulated HPA axis is essential for overall physical and mental health.

When being mindful of ikigai, the brain likely favours a combination of alpha, theta, and gamma brain waves, depending on the specific state of mind and activity associated with contemplating or engaging in one's sense of purpose.

ALPHA BRAIN WAVES (8-13 HZ): CALM AND REFLECTIVE STATES

When you are contemplating what gives your life meaning or simply enjoying small, meaningful moments, alpha waves help calm the mind and reduce stress.

Being mindful of ikigai often involves a balance between relaxation and focus, a state conducive to alpha wave activity.

THETA BRAIN WAVES (4-8 HZ): CREATIVITY AND INTUITION

Theta waves support imaginative processes when envisioning your purpose or considering new ways to align with your values and passions. They are also active during moments of self-reflection or spiritual connection, which are key to uncovering deeper aspects of ikigai.

BETA BRAIN WAVES (13-30 HZ): PROBLEM-SOLVING

When you're strategizing or engaging in focused tasks to achieve your purpose, beta waves support concentration and problem-solving. However, excessive beta wave activity (associated with stress) might inhibit the reflective and intuitive aspects of ikigai.

GAMMA BRAIN WAVES (30-100 HZ): INTEGRATION AND FOCUS

When engaging deeply in meaningful activities—whether it's work, art, or community service—you may enter a "flow state", where gamma waves play a dominant role. Gamma waves also contribute to the integration of thoughts, emotions, and purpose, helping you experience a sense of fulfillment.

DOMINANT BRAIN WAVE STATES IN DIFFERENT IKIGAI-RELATED ACTIVITIES

ACTIVITY	DOMINANT BRAIN WAVES	WHY?
Reflecting on purpose and values	Alpha, Theta	Encourages calm introspection and creativity.
Deep engagement in meaningful tasks	Gamma	Supports flow states and integrated cognition.
Practicing mindfulness or gratitude	Alpha, Theta	Promotes relaxation, emotional regulation, and connection to the present.
Goal setting and problem-solving	Beta	Facilitates logical thinking and focused planning.

NEUROBIOLOGICAL BENEFITS OF PASSION AND PURPOSE (IKIGAI) BRAIN WAVE STATES

- *Stress Reduction*: Increased alpha and theta wave activity reduces the production of stress hormones (e.g., cortisol) and promotes relaxation.
- *Neuroplasticity*: Gamma and theta waves enhance the brain's ability to rewire and adapt, supporting personal growth and healing.
- *Emotional Resilience*: Balanced brain wave activity improves emotional regulation, fostering greater clarity and stability in pursuing your ikigai.

HOW TO CULTIVATE FAVOURABLE BRAIN WAVES FOR IKIGAI

1. *Mindfulness Meditation*: Increase alpha and theta waves, helping you reflect on your purpose and appreciate the present moment.
2. *Journaling and Gratitude Practices*: Boost alpha activity by encouraging introspection and emotional balance.

3. *Creative Activities*: Engage in hobbies or crafts that inspire theta and gamma waves.
4. *Flow-Inducing Tasks*: Participate in challenging but rewarding activities to activate gamma waves and deepen your connection to ikigai.

The balance of energy among the four elements of ikigai—what you love, what you're good at, what the world needs, and what you can be paid for—is not necessarily about equal distribution. Instead, it's about alignment and prioritization based on individual goals and circumstances.

Your energy is limited, so how you allocate it matters. However, the goal is not to evenly divide energy across the four elements but to create a balance that aligns with your values and needs. Your focus on each element can shift over time depending on personal and external factors, such as financial needs, passions, or societal demands.

Ikigai is less about strict equality among its elements and more about achieving synergy, where energy invested in one element complements the others. Time spent doing what you love can often improve what you're good at. Similarly, solving what the world needs might open opportunities for compensation. If one element consumes too much energy, it can diminish the synergy. For example, dedicating too much effort to earning might leave little energy for creativity, purpose, or personal growth. In certain phases of life, one element may need more attention (e.g., compensation during financial strain, or passion during a midlife crisis). Accepting this can help you focus without guilt. Activities that align with multiple elements can maximize energy efficiency.

For instance, if your work involves something you love and the world needs, it will feel less draining even if compensation is the focus. Periodically reassess your ikigai to ensure that energy allocation reflects your evolving goals and circumstances. What feels balanced now might not work in the future. If you're overinvested in one area (e.g., compensation), start introducing small actions that address neglected elements. For example, volunteering can address "what the world needs" without requiring a massive time commitment.

Let's say you prioritize compensation because of financial pressures: You take a higher-paying job that may not align fully with your passions or the world's needs. Initially, this reduces energy for other elements. With financial stability achieved, you shift focus to incorporating elements you love or developing skills. Over time, you strive to adjust your role or explore side projects that align with other aspects of ikigai. This dynamic approach prevents burnout while acknowledging the reality of finite energy.

Ikigai encourages living intentionally, focusing your energy on what matters most. Course correction ensures that your actions remain purposeful and aligned with this intentionality. Both approaches acknowledge that life is unpredictable, and success or fulfillment depends on your ability to adapt. By embracing course correction, you honor the evolving nature of ikigai and ensure that setbacks or changes become opportunities for growth. Together, they emphasize the importance of ongoing evaluation, adaptability, and refinement to stay aligned with your purpose, even as life changes. Just as the veteran blacksmith perfects their swing through constant adjustment, achieving and sustaining your ikigai requires regular recalibration of your actions.

CHAPTER 18

THE IMPORTANCE OF RECOVERY

By MASTERING RECOVERY, SEALs NOT ONLY PREVENT BURNOUT but ensure they return sharper, faster, and more resilient. It's a lesson for all of us: Recovery is not the opposite of progress; it's the foundation of it.

Recovery shouldn't wait until exhaustion hits; it starts with a proactive mindset that values preparation for the next challenge. By treating recovery as part of the mission itself, SEALs sustain their peak performance and readiness in even the most demanding environments.

In the context of brain wave formation, recovery is the process of guiding the brain from high-frequency states of activity, like beta waves, into slower, restorative states such as alpha, theta, and delta waves. While beta waves are essential for peak performance, prolonged time in this state can lead to mental fatigue and diminished efficiency. Recovery allows the brain to step back from this hyperalertness and transition into a more balanced rhythm.

In the spirit of cellular health leading to increased brain power, recovery is initiated by the brain's ability to shift attention and prioritize processes that facilitate restoration and equilibrium. When the brain is engaged in high-intensity tasks or stress, our brain cells become exhausted by processes that demand focus, coordination, and rapid response, often supported by beta-wave activity. Recovery begins when the brain deliberately or naturally redirects its focus to processes associated with relaxation, repair, and integration.

This redirection occurs when signals from competing neural systems—such as those involved in interoception (monitoring the body's internal state) or parasympathetic activity—become our center of attention. For example, after prolonged effort, signals of fatigue or stress from the body may "win" the competition for attention, prompting a conscious shift toward rest. In this way, recovery is initiated by the brain's ability to recognize and prioritize signals that suggest the need for restoration.

Once recovery processes are activated, the cells in our body begin to shift focus from external demands to emphasizing internal homeostasis. This allows the prefrontal cortex, which is heavily engaged during focused activity, to reduce its dominance, enabling slower and more diffuse neural networks, like those associated with the default mode network (DMN), to take over. The DMN is involved in introspection, memory consolidation, and creative problem-solving, which are essential for psychological and cognitive recovery.

Through practices such as mindfulness, meditation, or simply disengaging from stressors (going for a walk, let's say), the mind and energy focus is guided toward these restorative states. These practices amplify parasympathetic signals and foster the brain's natural recovery mechanisms, promoting alpha and theta brain wave activity. In this way, recovery is seen as a dynamic process of shifting attention and resources from task-oriented, high-energy states to those that support repair, reflection, and renewal. Science is now developing a much greater appreciation of the healing effects of the mind and the therapeutic benefits of being in different brain wave states.

It is possible to think yourself into different brain wave patterns to promote health and recovery, as the brain is highly responsive to intentional mental practices. Brain wave patterns are essentially the electrical rhythms of neural activity, and these rhythms can be influenced by the focus and quality of thought.

For instance, guided meditation often encourages a shift from beta waves, which are associated with alertness and stress, to alpha waves, linked to calmness and relaxation. By focusing on a single thought, like a calming mantra or visualization of a peaceful scene, the brain disengages from the rapid, high-frequency activity of stress or problem-solving. This shift reduces physiological arousal and fosters a state conducive to healing, as alpha waves promote a relaxed but alert mental state.

Even deeper states, associated with theta and delta waves, can be accessed through advanced meditation or practices like yoga nidra. Theta waves, common during light sleep or deep relaxation, support emotional healing, creativity, and problem-solving. Intentional activities such as deep visualization or daydreaming can encourage these brain waves, fostering recovery and rejuvenation. Delta waves, primarily associated with deep, restorative sleep, can be indirectly influenced through practices that prepare the mind for rest, such as presleep relaxation techniques or body scans, helping the body enter its most restorative phase.

Cognitive reframing and biofeedback also illustrate how intentional thought patterns can influence brain wave states. Biofeedback devices allow individuals to monitor their brain waves and adjust their mental states in real time, reinforcing the connection between thought and neural activity. By cultivating calm, positive, or focused thought patterns, individuals can actively influence their brain's electrical rhythms, enhancing recovery and promoting overall well-being.

In essence, the brain is not a passive system but a dynamic, adaptive organ that responds to mental input. By intentionally guiding thought processes toward relaxation, positivity, and focus, it is indeed possible to shift brain wave patterns, supporting health and recovery. This mind-body connection underscores the profound power of intentional mental practices in shaping physical and mental health.

I've just recently discovered how I can meditate and finally achieve significant periods without thoughts disrupting my focus on the present moment. I've managed this by not trying to think about nothing but instead trying to put all of my focus (all my cells aligned) on attempting to sense what my skin is experiencing. Instead of focusing on breathing or heart rate which fluctuates and seems to trigger thoughts very regularly with each change from inhale to exhale. When I focus on my skin, in a quiet dark environment, it's much more of a constant. It's also very energetic and I feel as though I can get all my cellular tissue to simply try to feel the background energy that is all around us. There is not a rhythm and instead it's a constant hum and it's much easier to get lost in it. Slowing my heart rate, breathing, and even experimenting with long breath holds as part of my free-diving training. It's extremely peaceful. Trying to think about nothing is still thinking. The key to meditation and creating larger gaps without thought is to take your focus out of your head and into your body parts.

CHAPTER 19

MY PROTOCOLS

TOP SCIENTISTS ARE STILL FIGURING OUT ALL FUNCTIONS OF mitochondria. But we know enough to determine that from a risk-to-reward perspective, we should do everything we can to take care of them.

Adam Smith's invisible hand theory is a fundamental concept in economics that describes how individual self-interest and competition in a free-market economy leads to the efficient allocation of resources. Like an unseen force, the invisible hand guides the overall market. This is a good analogy for the ten quadrillion mitochondria each of us carries within our bodies that busily undertake tasks in every cell. Our job is to get them the right ingredients to do their jobs well. This includes working our cardiovascular systems to circulate all the supplies we give them and getting them ample oxygen. We just need to give them the opportunity to do their many jobs. If we do that, our mitochondria adjust their function in response to each cell's energy needs autonomously and without central planning. Competition in the marketplace has them changing size, shape, form, and function to provide different services. Providing only the basic services isn't enough—we need to make sure they are healthy and plentiful so they can provide all their maintenance and specialized services for us. If they have to spend all their time struggling to just produce energy, they won't be able to do other jobs, like keeping the heart and other organs operating properly.

Like competition in capitalism, mitophagy ensures survival of the fittest. Autophagy is the selection and recycling or elimination of degraded or damaged cells. Mitophagy is part of that process; it's the body's mitochondrial cleanup and recycling program. Through mitophagy, old, damaged, and dysfunctional mitochondria are recycled or eliminated. Think of this as quality control by "thinning the herd". Certain proteins in our cells flag the weak mitochondria for destruction, then other specialized cell parts move in and perform the breakdown and cleanup of the weak mitochondria. The waste from this process is removed and the key materials are recycled. This is a very neat and efficient process when all is working as it should. I like this biological-based way to a healthier lifespan because human-engineered interventions oftentimes have unseen consequences.

The big takeaway here is you must take care of your mitochondria so they can take care of you. As I learned more about mitochondria and took steps to repair mine, my energy exploded. I started with an eight-week mitochondrial reset. Eight weeks of whole foods, no added sugar, and no alcohol was the reboot my biological supercomputer needed.

Suddenly, I wasn't riding the short-term glucose waves. I could go for days without needing a lot of food, or even fast for many days, because my energy was so high. Previously, the idea of going without a meal for twenty-four hours would have me picturing myself starving in the fetal position. But with healthier mitochondria, my body's ability to tap its energy stores seems limitless. My physical energy, strength, and endurance has skyrocketed.

Even at age fifty-four, I felt better than I had over a decade earlier. It wasn't about getting older or lacking willpower. It was that my lifestyle had resulted in a terribly weak dysfunctional energy system. Once repaired, I felt freed. I was energized with excitement to make more improvements. I lost all cravings and instead developed an aversion to eating unhealthy foods, drinking, and just sitting around "relaxing". When focusing inward, I realized, my very cells actually became wired with strong aversion to my old habits. I looked forward to eating better and doing more. I enjoyed challenging myself to see what else I could do. I swear, I never dreamed that I would feel such a strong change in my preferences.

Again, this isn't a recipe book. I am not telling you what to do; I am outlining the analytic tools I have employed both in my career and now in my health journey in the hopes you will develop what works best for you. Aging gracefully has many different paths. For example, Hong Kong has one of the longest male life expectancies and is one of the largest per-capita consumers of meat in the world. Spain, France, and Italy often top life-expectancy charts and don't have strict diet and exercise protocols or much different tobacco-use percentages. But this is what is working for me.

INCREASING CARDIO CAPACITY

Detailed styles of training can include targeting heart rates for extended durations. Some people aim for a particular zone, getting their heartbeat to a certain rate and maintaining that rate for a particular amount of time. Likewise, there are different theories about when you should eat and what you should eat before and after a workout. My advice is to do what works for you, but don't get in a rut. Try out different things. Mix it up. If you're doing only short, high-intensity workouts, try some longer duration exercises in lower heart rate zones, like light hiking, jogging, and bike riding. They can also be time consuming, but I was intrigued to look for alternatives that might be quicker and yield similar returns.

Right now, high-intensity workouts like high-intensity interval training (HIIT) are popular. Clinical studies have proven this kind of workout drains all the energy from our cells, sending a strong signal that spurs mitochondrial growth. Along those same lines, new workout styles have been developed where you push for the absolute maximum degree of intensity possible for very short durations—even just twenty to thirty seconds. I like this style, partly because I struggle to commit ample time to working out, but I do enjoy sports that entail short bursts of high energy.

I'd heard of VO2 max testing for high-performance sports like ski racing and for elite hockey players but was unaware of how important the measure was. VO2 max is a measure of the maximum amount of oxygen that our body can consume during intense exercise. This measurement is an indicator of how well your heart, lungs, and entire cardiovascular system can work together to deliver oxygen to your blood vessels, which in turn delivers oxygen to your other cells, including those that make up your muscles. It's also influenced by our mitochondria's ability to produce energy. VO2 max testing is an effective way of measuring our overall aerobic capacity.

It's also a great measure for tracking how well we are aging. A healthy young person's VO2 max is very high, but as we age, it decreases, typically declining around 5–10 per cent per decade after the age of thirty. This corresponds with the diminishing functionality it measures. Another simple way to look at VO2 max is as a measure of our body's ability to produce energy. Our bodies need energy to grow and repair themselves, and when they don't have enough, they have to make tough decisions, prioritizing where to send that energy that's in short supply. If your body's using all the energy to maintain basic functions, you won't have enough to heal damaged tissue. Increasing VO2 max is very difficult if levels fall too low. With dedication to the best protocols, we are able to slow the natural decline and even reverse it.

Allowing our bodies' maintenance functions to deteriorate is like not changing a car's engine oil or allowing the brakes or the shocks to wear out. Poor maintenance can lead to a single point of failure that results in a costly breakdown or a deadly accident. Severe malfunctions can leave key components beyond repair.

Fortunately, there's much we can do to help ourselves. With regular exercise, you can improve your VO2 max and look forward to a longer, healthier life. There are other auxiliary benefits worth mentioning, like staving off impotency and avoiding spending your final years in a diaper.

GROWING LEAN MUSCLE MASS

Physical activity strengthens your muscles, improves your cardiovascular system, boosts your mood, enhances your flexibility, supports weight management, and increases your metabolism and mitochondrial health and density, all while reducing the risk of chronic diseases like heart disease, diabetes, and obesity. Physical activity promotes better quality of life as you age, and even lowers the odds of slip and falls, which often correlate to a quick demise later in life.

Recently, muscle mass has been found to play a significant role in immunity. Muscles store immune cells, which are released to defend against foreign pathogens. They also release myokines during exercise, which enhances the immune response with an anti-inflammatory effect. This combines to combat and maintain overall health. This is a great reason to keep working out and developing muscle mass as you age. Otherwise, you'll have trouble fighting off infections and illnesses.

What's important for me is that I want to groom the habit of doing something every day. The importance is habit and consistency, not intensity. It can be a simple as a thirty-second plank or a leisurely walk after dinner. Starting a daily exercise routine, whatever it is, will help you develop and maintain a habit that pays off now and in the future. What you do—whether it's walking, biking, lifting weights, or playing an organized sport—is less important than doing something regularly.

Exercise is more than a stress reliever or creator of a good physical foundation for brain health. Exercise literally manufactures brain food. Lactate.

I used to think of lactate as the enemy—the source of that burning sensation in muscles during intense exercise. Like most, I had bought into the old story that lactate was simply a waste product to be endured. The truth revolutionized my understanding of body-brain connection: Lactate isn't waste at all, but premium brain fuel. When you push your body—whether sprinting or lifting—your muscles produce lactate that crosses the blood-brain barrier, where your brain actually prefers it to glucose. This isn't just about energy; lactate triggers a cascade of benefits including enhanced neural plasticity, improved learning capacity, and sharper memory formation. It's nature's own cognitive enhancer, produced right in your own body.

This explains the post-exercise mental clarity that feels like someone wiping clean a dusty window in your mind. During physical exertion, your brain isn't just along for the ride—it's actively participating in a sophisticated energy exchange. The lactate produced by your muscles becomes a signaling molecule for brain function, promoting neurogenesis (the formation of new neurons) and reducing neuroinflammation.

It even supports microangiogenesis—the formation of new blood vessels in your brain. It's a beautiful irony that the very substance once blamed for limiting performance is actually key to enhancing it, not just physically but mentally. Every workout isn't just building stronger muscles; it's feeding your brain its preferred fuel source.

FASTING

I was amazed to learn how important fasting is for health. When you research this subject, which I highly recommend, you come to realize why it has become a significant practice in many religious traditions. I have little doubt that this stems from the fact that early humans saw a correlation where people who hadn't eaten for a while didn't get sick as often as those who ate regularly. It's probable the tradition of fasting has deep roots in hunter-gatherer societies long before the written word. Early humans undoubtedly had to regularly manage their way through extended periods with little or no food and would have surely developed an intimate understanding of fasting.

Both intermittent and extended fasting have short-term and long-term health benefits. In addition to helping people quickly get to their ideal weight, fasting also triggers a process called *autophagy*, where the body clears out damaged cells, supporting the cellular renewal process. This reduces the risk of certain diseases. Fasting has also been linked to cancer-fighting effects because it appears to inhibit tumor growth while promoting apoptosis, or cell death, in cancer cells.

There's mounting evidence that fasting reduces the risk of cancer and slows the spread of cancer cells. It may even improve the effectiveness of chemotherapy. Clinical studies show we can lessen the risk of recurrence by engaging in periods of intermittent fasting during recovery following cancer treatments.

There are many benefits from shortening our eating window, allowing more time between the last and first meals of each day. Eat your last meal earlier and/or your first meal later to allow a minimum of sixteen hours between these meals. This provides the gut with ample time needed to repair itself, which reduces inflammation and leads to improved gut health, essential for longevity.

Better gut health can help lessen or cure diseases like irritable bowel syndrome (IBS), ulcers, Crohn's disease, and leaky gut. Giving your gut that break allows it to repair and replace its damaged cells and strengthen its lining and defenses.

Fasting also promotes the production of melatonin, a hormone crucial in regulating sleep patterns, maintaining circadian rhythms, and improving sleep quality.

Fasting and melatonin production trigger mitophagy, which is when we remove damaged mitochondria. New mitochondria are then produced by fission, where they divide to create more mitochondria. Fasting helps to optimize cellular function, potentially slowing down the aging process altogether.

Extended and intermittent fasting have been shown to stimulate the release of stem cells, which can aid in tissue regeneration repair and overall rejuvenation attributing to improved longevity. I've experimented with extended fasting, subsisting for as long as 122 hours—just over five days—on black coffee, water with electrolytes, and green tea. I plan to repeat this every year to continue reaping the health benefits, including reducing the risk of cancer, and it's also said to help maintain a youthful appearance. Fasting also limits the negative effects of reactive oxygen species (ROS), combats age-related decline, supports cardiovascular health, and protects against neurodegenerative diseases.

Fasting promotes molecular synthesis, and it also boosts sirtuin production. Sirtuins (SIRTs) are proteins that play a critical role in regulating cellular processes, including gene expression, DNA repair, metabolism, and longevity. Sirtuins are referred to as "longevity proteins" due to their involvement in promoting cellular health and increasing life span. Sirtuin-related therapies now in development could reverse the aging process. Experiments on mice have turned gray fur to black and reversed glaucoma, restoring sight. Some experts predict that sirtuins may eventually be used in treatments to stave off the effects of aging in humans by several decades or more.

Sirtuins help repair DNA, reduce inflammation, enhance stress resistance, and contribute to overall health. In addition to fasting, you can also increase sirtuin production by eating foods rich in resveratrol, such as grapes and berries. Scientists have identified seven different sirtuins, each with specialized body maintenance functions.

Telomeres are protective chromosome caps that appear to shorten as we age. Sirtuins are believed to influence or maintain telomere length. This area of research appears to have so much promise with anti-aging therapies that it could soon lead to the most significant medical breakthroughs in history. I believe that we will see the average life expectancy increase more than it ever has in history, with far-reaching implications.

Again, studies are being done, and some have even identified a single molecule that we produce that lengthens our telomeres. Clinical studies are being done to prove its effectiveness at reversing aging, curing neurodegenerative diseases, and even curing cancers. What we won't know for decades is what happens to people's long-term health when you increase levels of one molecule we naturally produce.

In the meantime, we have a very good understanding how to support sirtuin health and keep our telomeres ideal. We've pretty much covered it all with our early review of a healthy diet, fasting, exercise, sleep, and stress management. Note how the basic principles of eating natural foods, engaging in natural movement and respecting our natural body rhythms seems to be the answer for pretty much everything. This makes a lot of sense because it's simply living with respect for our evolutionary history and the deep knowledge that's developed into every cell in our bodies. When we take care of the basics, our cells and their parts take care of us.

Fasting is working for me but it's not for everyone, nor does it have to be. I can tell you it does get easier. At the beginning not eating alarms the body and it fights back by ramping up hunger pangs. My advice is that if you are thinking of fasting start by lowering your sugar and alcohol intake in advance. And slow and steady does win the race. Small permanent changes will beat intense less-permanent ones. A lot of the negative feelings associated with starting fasting come from coming clean from booze and sugar. By reducing the glucose spikes beforehand, fasting becomes surprisingly easy.

NUTRITIONAL STRATEGIES AND SUPPLEMENTS FOR BETTER MITOCHONDRIAL FUNCTION

Consuming foods high in antioxidants such as berries, nuts, and green leafy vegetables protect the mitochondria from damage caused by free radicals. The fatty acids found in fish oil and flax seeds all support mitochondrial membrane health and enhance energy production. Coenzyme q10 (CoQ10) supplements have been shown to improve mitochondrial function and energy production, and recent studies have found that a substance found in pomegranates and other foods is beneficial for mitochondrial health.

Unfortunately, due to microbial damage, even when we digest foods that are beneficial, our bodies often aren't able to absorb the nutrients. Magnesium supports mitochondrial health and energy production and is essential for over three hundred biochemical reactions. It can be supplemented with most electrolyte drink packs.

A ketogenic diet, which is low in carbohydrates and high in healthy fats and protein, increases the number of mitochondria and makes cells more efficient as they produce energy.

The dietary change alone should be made gradually; it takes mental energy to make the shift and stick to this new plan. For many people, simply eating better is enough. Getting your diet right allows you to see a change quickly. By gradually introducing more ketogenic elements while eliminating glucose dependency with fruits, nuts, eggs, and avocados in the morning, followed by proteins and vegetables later in the day, and then reducing your eating window, you will seriously enhance your fat-burning capabilities. Listen to your body. Not everyone can start with intense activities right away on their health journey. Stretching, yoga, and light walks may be more appropriate, but the idea is to start doing little things every day. Be mindful about starting down the healthy path, building small habits along the way. Pushing too hard too soon can lead to discouragement and physical pain or injury. Self-compassion is better, and your first week should be about being kind to yourself, recognizing your body's current limits, and gradually building up stamina and health. Incorporating nutrients like CoQ10, omega-3s, and antioxidants will help with mitochondria function, then regular, moderate exercise will continue the process. Building these habits will stimulate mitochondrial biogenesis, improving their health function and increasing their numbers. And remember to get enough rest.

I know that this sounds like a lot, but the results have been dramatic, and ease with which the changes occurred made the experience vastly better than my past efforts to find better health. At the end of the day it's most important to find new choices you enjoy that improve mitochondria health. For dietary choices it really requires two things: (1) Restrict added sugar or foods that spike your glucose levels. (2) Restrict or better yet eliminate all ultra-processed food.

IS ULTRA-PROCESSED FOOD ZOMBIE FOOD?

Our brain's feel-good chemical factory has a crucial raw material problem: It can't manufacture serotonin without tryptophan, an essential amino acid that only comes from your diet. Think of tryptophan as the master key that unlocks not just your mood, but fifteen vital functions serotonin provides in your brain—from appetite control to sleep regulation, from cognitive clarity to emotional resilience.

When you eat whole, natural foods rich in tryptophan, you're providing your body with the building blocks it needs for optimal neurochemical production. But here's where modern eating habits throw a wrench in the works: Ultra-processed foods, while calorically dense, are often stripped of bioavailable tryptophan. They're essentially "zombie fuel"—providing enough energy to keep you moving, but starving your brain of the essential nutrients it needs for higher-level thinking and emotional regulation.

The process is fascinating: Tryptophan doesn't just influence serotonin production. It's also a precursor for melatonin (your sleep hormone) and niacin (vitamin B3). When you're running low on tryptophan, it creates a domino effect. Your brain's ability to produce these vital neurochemicals diminishes, affecting everything from your sleep quality to your stress resilience. It's like trying to run a sophisticated factory with subpar raw materials—the end products will inevitably be compromised.

Consider this: While processed foods might give you a quick energy boost, they're often lacking the complex amino acid profiles found in whole foods. Your body is left with enough fuel to move, but not enough raw materials to maintain optimal brain chemistry. This may explain why people who consume primarily processed foods often report feeling mentally foggy, emotionally flat, or disconnected—their brains are literally running on empty when it comes to these essential building blocks of consciousness.

I do want to say when it comes to booze—while alcohol might seem like a quick path to feeling good—it actually wreaks havoc on your tryptophan-serotonin system. When you drink, alcohol forces your liver to prioritize its metabolism over proper tryptophan processing, creating a biochemical traffic jam that disrupts your entire serotonin production system. This explains why the temporary lift in mood from drinking comes at such a steep biological price—you're essentially borrowing tomorrow's happiness at a punishing interest rate.

The morning-after blues aren't just about dehydration; they're a direct result of this tryptophan-serotonin disruption. Your brain, having been flooded with alcohol-induced serotonin release, now struggles to maintain proper neurotransmitter balance. This biochemical chaos manifests as anxiety, depression, and irritability—creating a temptation to drink again to relieve these symptoms. It's a vicious cycle that not only depletes your natural serotonin production but also compromises your brain's ability to effectively use the tryptophan you get from food.

SLEEP

Chronic stress and lack of adequate sleep negatively impact mitochondrial health. Aligning your sleep with your circadian rhythm by being active during the daylight hours and sleeping in the dark plays a big role in melatonin production, which is needed to rest and replenish your mitochondria. Melatonin, a naturally produced sleep aid, is key to the mitochondria biogenesis process. Excessive alcohol consumption and smoking can lead to mitochondrial dysfunction. Smoking and even vaping distributes toxins throughout the body, while alcohol is basically ethanol/sugar, and the more you limit your intake, the better for your health. Entire books have been written on this subject, and the bottom line is that smoking and alcohol are poisonous to your body. Whatever it does for you in the short term, it does the opposite for you in the long term. Alcohol, I believe, is one of the biggest life traps going these days. Too often we casually develop a habit of letting alcohol consumption lead to dropping good habits.

It's far too easy to get carried away in the moment of a late-night celebration only to find yourself drained of energy the next day and therefore deciding to sleep in and do less activity. Bit by bit, this habit can get reinforced such that years go by, and we find ourselves lacking the energy and physical abilities to do those activities that give us strength. It's counterintuitive to think that exercising increases your energy but this principle needs to become second nature, just like understanding when being a contrarian investor is needed to protect your portfolio's health and build on gains.

Low light levels before bed followed by uninterrupted sleep are required to not disrupt normal melatonin production. Proper melatonin production is vital. It causes our brains to shrink each night thereby enabling our brain's lymphatic drainage system to clear out harmful toxins. Consider the painful headaches associated with brain inflammation from a bad hangover. Respecting our circadian rhythms and need for melatonin production reduces the odds of many serious neural degenerative diseases like Alzheimer's, Parkinson's, and dementia, while cleaning up and eliminating toxic misfolded proteins.

Quality sleep provides many benefits, supporting various psychological processes and contributing to overall health and longevity. It's also key to learning, memory storage, and maintaining a positive mood. We all know how difficult day-to-day function can be when we're sleep deprived. Military interrogators have long experimented with sleep deprivation as a torture technique to wear people down and break their spirits. So, let's try not to torture ourselves.

SAUNAS

Given my maternal Finnish background, it's not surprising I have a deep love for saunas. My appreciation is definitely epigenetically programmed as Finland leads the world with about 3.3 million saunas for its 5.5 million people. Scientific studies are showing the benefits of using a sauna for your cardiovascular system with data showing three to four times a week yields significant benefits. Some people even compare it to jogging and other exercises—it's that good for you.

Sitting in a sauna boosts your immune system, aids cellular repair, and generates those all-important heat shock proteins (also known as chaperone proteins). Heat in general, including steam rooms and hot springs, can be very relaxing and provide health benefits. Natural hot springs have the added benefit of a variety of minerals.

If you don't have the time or budget to enjoy a sauna, steam room, or hot spring, try a hot bath with some mineral additives.

COLD PLUNGES

After enjoying the heat, finish with cold. The heat opens your pores, flushing out the toxins, and the cold closes them, enhances our immune system, and gives us a serious endorphin rush. A cold finish could be a cold plunge, a cold shower, an ice bath, or an outdoor polar dip. Cold plunging actually produces even more heat shock proteins (HSPs) than heat treatments, which are beneficial for combating inflammation issues.

Some people complain about not enjoying the cold, but again, the "use it or lose it" rule applies. If we avoid the cold, we will never develop the ability to withstand it or enjoy its health benefits. Just a few minutes in ice water helps encourage our bodies to burn fat and generate heat, as well as send more oxygen and nutrients to our extremities. If we do this on a regular basis, we grow more capillaries for carrying even more oxygen-rich blood to our hands and fingers.

I utilize both hot and cold treatments, and I really stepped up my treatments after reading two books, *The Way of the Iceman* about Wim Hof and Koen de Jong and *Breath* by James Nestor. When I first started my health journey, these were the therapies that kickstarted my energy boost. I could feel a difference in my energy almost immediately.

I like starting my day with a cold plunge because I feel it makes other healthy choices easier. It wakes you up and makes you present in dramatic fashion. Combined with some power breathing techniques, you'll feel a huge energy boost. Estimates are that some people see a 250 per cent dopamine boost from a serious cold plunge. I really credit cold plunges for helping me stay energized and focused on my health journey.

During my first few weeks of cutting out alcohol and sugar I found that a dunk in my cold plunge completely eliminated my cravings as the sauna/cold plunge combo gave me a rush of pain-killing beta-endorphins and mood-enhancing norepinephrine, a dopamine reward and serotonin boost for anti-stress mood positivity. Evidence suggests that the Finns have instinctively known this as sauna bathing and rolling in the snow has been a cultural practice for thousands of years.

MODERN TECH

Pulsed Electromagnetic Field (PEMF) mats which produce different magnetic frequencies have been developed as a modern way to promote healing and wellness while regulating our neurochemicals. Because our bodies operate on different frequencies, it's been shown that some improve sleep, concentration, or mood, or can have an overall grounding effect. The mats trigger various brain waves and stimulate cellular repair. The scientific proof supporting the benefits of these mats is in the early stages, but I've experienced excellent results with them, especially when I use them in conjunction with red light therapy.

This is especially helpful in winter when the days are shorter and access to natural sunlight is limited. Conditions such as seasonal affective disorder (SAD) depression may be treated with this type of therapy. Just like the sauna and cold plunge, PEMF and red light therapy devices boost our pain-killer endorphins, serotonin, and dopamine, but also have been shown to boost brain-nurturing melatonin and nitric oxide, which improves blood flow and reduces inflammation. All the above therapies are great and when doing them, I also focus on my breathing, heart rate, and my thoughts.

I am pretty excited about how AI training equipment is going to weave itself into the health process. The advantage of using AI technology here is that it can learn what your maximum abilities are, and then push you to that maximum, with adaptive resistance. So, when you stop pushing on a machine, it doesn't push back, eliminating the majority of typical injury risk. Also, it can provide resistance from many different angles, working all our muscles to the max from every direction.

I balance high- and low-intensity physical workouts with rest and meditation too. I push myself to grow mentally and physically. I try to find ways into the flow state and enjoy the neurochemical rushes that make one feel so good.

BREATH WORK AND MEDITATION

Over time, you'll discover many new habits that pair well with breath work and meditation, and they will become part of your routine. Adding calendar appointments, well-placed sticky notes, or choosing an app that reminds you to take these breaks will help ensure you form the habit sooner. Being proactive, instead of waiting until the symptoms of stress appear, could ward off stress you didn't know was building up.

I've been lucky to get to know some high-performance and professional athletes and trainers. They've often talked about the benefits of targeted training goals. Since starting my health journey, I've ramped up my hiking, biking, and swimming, and started training for free diving—not for the crazy depths, but so I can go for long swims over reefs and catch lobster by hand. I'm hoping this kind of training will increase my lung capacity and improve my VO2 max. Free-diving training can increase your lung capacity by 50 to 70 per cent, and that can't be a bad thing!

Part of the free-diving training combines yoga, stretching, and breath work. Imagine your lungs as two balloons. Inhale deeply, filling them all the way up, then stretch to one side, flexing your ribs and pushing your lungs out. Try to force all the air to one side of your chest and then the other. The idea is to use your muscles to breathe so you're breathing more deeply and fully. You might have a tight chest and have never tried to make the most of your lung capacity. Free-diving training enhances lung function, increases carbon dioxide tolerance, improves diaphragm strength, and lowers our resting heart rate. Seems to me like the training is worth pursuing just for the health benefits even if you never get in the ocean.

For those who are interested in doing the eight-week mitochondria reset, here is a bit more of an outline.

WEEKS 1-2: CLEARING THE GROUND AND RESETTING THE BASICS

During the first two weeks, the focus is on detoxifying your body and creating the optimal conditions for mitochondrial repair. The process begins with eliminating dietary and environmental stressors that impair mitochondrial function, such as refined sugars, processed foods. Your meals should center around high-quality proteins from sources like grass-fed beef, pasture-raised poultry, wild-caught fish, and eggs. These proteins provide the building blocks for cellular repair and enzymes crucial for mitochondrial function. Plant-based proteins like lentils, chickpeas, and tempeh can also contribute to a balanced intake, especially when paired with other nutrient-rich foods. A good rule of thumb is the food you eat during the reset should have an ingredient list of one item. The focus is on whole foods.

Healthy fats are another cornerstone of the mitochondria reset diet. Avocados, extra virgin olive oil, nuts, seeds, and fatty fish such as salmon and mackerel deliver essential omega-3 fatty acids and monounsaturated fats. These fats are not only anti-inflammatory but also essential for maintaining the structural integrity of mitochondrial membranes, which are vital for energy production.

Vegetables should dominate your plate, especially dark, leafy greens like kale, spinach, and Swiss chard. These are rich in magnesium, a critical cofactor in many mitochondrial processes. Cruciferous vegetables like broccoli, cauliflower, and Brussels sprouts contain sulfur compounds that help detoxify and support mitochondrial health. Brightly colored vegetables and fruits, such as bell peppers, carrots, and berries, are packed with antioxidants like vitamin C, polyphenols, and flavonoids that combat oxidative stress and prevent mitochondrial damage.

Prebiotic foods like garlic, onions, leeks, and asparagus nourish your gut microbiome, which has a direct impact on mitochondrial health through the gut-mitochondria axis. These foods support the production of short-chain fatty acids, which enhance energy metabolism and reduce inflammation. Fermented foods, such as sauerkraut, kimchi, and yogurt, help populate your gut with beneficial bacteria, further reinforcing this connection.

Carbohydrate intake should be moderate and come from whole, unprocessed sources like sweet potatoes, quinoa, and legumes. These provide a steady energy supply without causing blood sugar spikes, which can strain mitochondrial function. Avoid refined carbohydrates, as they contribute to inflammation and oxidative stress, undermining the reset process.

Hydration is also crucial, so aim to drink plenty of water throughout the day. You might also incorporate herbal teas like green tea, which is rich in EGCG, a compound known to support mitochondrial biogenesis and function. Bone broth is another excellent addition, as it provides amino acids and minerals that aid in cellular repair.

Spices and herbs like turmeric, ginger, rosemary, and oregano can amplify the benefits of your diet. Turmeric, for instance, contains curcumin, which is a powerful anti-inflammatory and supports mitochondrial health. Ginger aids digestion and reduces inflammation, while rosemary and oregano deliver polyphenols that protect cells from oxidative stress.

As inflammation decreases, you might notice subtle improvements in your energy levels, digestion, and mental clarity. The early cognitive effects stem from a reduction in systemic inflammation, which frees up neural resources and begins to enhance focus and cognitive sharpness.

WEEKS 3-4: ACTIVATING CELLULAR RENEWAL
AND ENHANCING RESILIENCE

By weeks three and four, your body is primed to take on more advanced strategies for mitochondrial repair and renewal. Intermittent fasting is introduced, with daily fasting windows of fourteen to sixteen hours. This practice stimulates mitophagy, a natural process where damaged mitochondria are broken down and cleared from cells. In tandem, cold exposure through practices like cold showers or ice baths, as well as heat exposure in saunas, trains your mitochondria to adapt to stressors, making them more resilient and efficient in energy production.

At this stage, the improvements in your microbiome become more pronounced. The gut lining continues to heal, aided by the production of short-chain fatty acids from prebiotic fibers. This strengthens the gut-mitochondria axis, a key connection in maintaining metabolic and immune health. On a cognitive level, your brain begins to benefit from enhanced mitochondrial energy output, which improves neural connectivity and supports better integration of sensory and cognitive input. This aligns with the science, proving healthier and more efficient brain networks lead to improved focus, clearer thinking, and a sense of heightened awareness.

WEEKS 5-6: ACCELERATING ENERGY
PRODUCTION AND DEEP REPAIR

The fifth and sixth weeks represent the most transformative phase of the reset. Your mitochondria are now more resilient and ready for biogenesis, the creation of new mitochondria. High-intensity interval training (HIIT) and resistance exercises are introduced to stimulate this process. These activities challenge your cells to produce more energy, further enhancing mitochondrial density and efficiency. Anti-inflammatory pathways are fully activated by this point, leading to significantly reduced oxidative stress and cellular damage.

The microbiome also reaches a state of synergy with your mitochondria. A well-diversified gut microbiome helps regulate inflammation and supports the production of key metabolites that further improve mitochondrial function. You may feel a dramatic boost in physical energy and mental sharpness. This is where many people report a deeper connection to their emotions and a heightened ability to process complex thoughts, as our ability to focus becomes more controlled and efficient. The integration of brain networks allows for richer, more expansive cognitive experiences, making this phase particularly impactful.

WEEKS 7-8: FULL OPTIMIZATION AND LASTING VITALITY

The final phase of the mitochondria reset is about locking in the gains and optimizing your body's energy system for long-term health. By now, your mitochondria are operating at peak efficiency, and your body has adapted to manage stressors with ease. The combination of clean energy production and reduced oxidative stress translates into sustained vitality and resilience. At this stage, your daily routines, such as nutrient-dense eating, fasting, and strategic exercise, feel natural and integrated into your lifestyle.

The microbiome, now thriving and diverse, works in harmony with your mitochondria, creating a feedback loop that supports metabolic health, immune function, and emotional stability. You may notice profound mental clarity, a sense of balance, and even creative breakthroughs. The enhanced connectivity between brain regions facilitated by optimized mitochondrial function allows for a more integrated and expansive sense of self, aligning with the principles of the maximum cellular health leading to peak cognitive performance. This phase feels like a culmination of the work you've put in—your body and mind functioning in harmony at their full potential.

The temptation to turn to big pharma instead of lifestyle modification is very real and promoted by various capitalist elements for sure. It's a big business and even though I am a big believer in modern medicine for major medical issues, I don't think modern medicine and the pharmaceutical industry are best for daily health maintenance.

In North America, medical students typically receive limited formal education in nutrition as part of their medical training. On average, medical schools provide around twenty to twenty-four hours of nutrition education over the course of the entire curriculum, which is only a small fraction of the total hours dedicated to other subjects.

Remember, medical school is typically four years, and in that entire time they spend less than a workweek on nutrition. Furthermore, this training often focuses on biochemistry and the role of nutrients in metabolic pathways rather than practical dietary counseling or the application of nutrition in managing chronic diseases. Also, this nutrition education is often integrated into broader subjects like physiology or pharmacology, rather than being a stand-alone course. As a result, many physicians report feeling underprepared to provide comprehensive nutritional guidance to their patients.

To me, interventions with pharmaceuticals are like subsidies. How often do we see all sorts of problems when our government takes steps that distort the market by subsidizing products? Subsidized corn, for example, became a chief source of food "energy" in the form of fructose or corn syrup. We see these ingredients in countless products as a cheap alternative to healthy, whole food choices. Likewise, these subsidized ingredients end up in animal feed to fatten the animals, versus alternative grass-fed and healthier free-range alternatives. Subsidized food pushing out other choices affects the marketplace, affects the planet, and damages our health.

FIND BALANCE

I like to think of health management as having a lot in common with financial management. Consider the risk-reward ratio and seek out low-risk investments for your body that provide high returns. Avoid big drawdown risks that could be hard to recover from.

It can be tempting to push too hard physically, thinking you'll have immediate, major gains. But your body doesn't work that way. When you exercise or change your diet, the physical gains are small and incremental, but with patience and regularity, they build safely over time. This is especially true if you're trying to recover from an injury. Work toward a safe goal and avoid future major losses or setbacks. Take small steps outside of your comfort zone and see how your health improves over time. Develop and maintain lifelong health habits.

If you're struggling to come back from an injury, do some research and see what other people have endured and how they recovered and even went on to do amazing things. David Goggins, for example, writes about how, even though he had seriously compromised knees, he went on to run ultramarathons. Reading about his comeback got me to shut up about my knee pain and figure out how to rehabilitate the joints. This ability-focused approach to my knee pain—focus on creating small stackable knee health habits—lowers the need to "get pumped up" to exercise. As my knee pain subsided, I needed less motivation to turn fitness prompts into action.

Goggins also helped me train my thoughts: I'd remind myself about his belief that we first think of giving up at only 40 per cent of our ability and I could keep going. Just by reframing my mind, I changed what I was capable of and got a much better workout.

Our bodies are always trying to conserve energy, and they will tell us it's time to stop when we have much more to give. This is why team sports or having a coach can make you work so much harder. Being surrounded by people pushing you to do more helps quiet that voice that's urging you to take a break.

Another inspiration for me has been NHL player Gary Roberts, who suffered a serious herniated disc in his neck that required surgery. Roberts was told he should never play hockey again. The risks were said to be too high and if he got hit hard, his neck could be compromised beyond repair, leaving him paralyzed. Instead of quitting, he built up his neck muscles, came back, and had a very long career in the NHL. Not only did he come back, but he also played hard, like the same gritty contact player he was before the injury. In retirement, he went on to help train and rehabilitate other NHL players like Steven Stamkos.

Find workouts you enjoy, and you'll be more likely to do them regularly. Look for the small gains that lead to big long-term benefits and make sure to generate the habit-forming reward chemicals. Consistency is more important than intensity. Even if it's limited to just putting on workout clothes, that is a tiny habit that can grow.

The journey toward optimum energy levels is not about willpower. It's about working smarter, adopting better strategies, and making better lifestyle choices that are both efficient and enjoyable. I know I keep repeating this, but to me it is so important. People start changing, rely on intensity and willpower, and yo-yo back. Studies suggest that 80–95 per cent of people who lose weight through willpower-driven diets regain it within one to five years. Up to two-thirds actually put more weight back on. Fifty per cent of new exercisers quit within six months. Small stackable habits that become automatic is the most energy-efficient way to make change.

In that regard, adopting this compassionate understanding and approach to starting your health journey is essential. Acknowledging the biological changes that individuals may face due to mitochondrial and liver health and adjusting strategies accordingly can be a more supportive and effective path forward for achieving long-term health and fitness goals. Mitochondria dysfunction leads to inefficient energy production, making it harder for the body to sustain prolonged physical activities. Liver health plays a critical role in managing energy reserves, especially glycogen storage and release. Poor liver health can impair this balance, contributing to a quicker onset of fatigue. You must be patient with yourself. Like I have said, progress is seldom a straight line, in finance as well as for your mind and body.

But if we properly prioritize our health in the present, we won't have to avoid life's challenging hills. We'll be prepared, see them coming, building momentum on approach. We'll become wired to seeking out hills and mountains, eagerly, with hunger. Our challenges will make our life more enjoyable and make us feel more alive. Stoke your curiosity, passion, and purpose and keep learning more about the possibilities. Hunt for bigger and better challenges. This is the path to epiphany. This is the evolutionary track to true happiness.

CHAPTER 20

SURFING THE SYSTEM

MY FRIEND SPENT SOME TIME IN LA, AND HE USED TO TAKE his kids surfing every morning. It was a habit he wanted to support for his then twelve- and fifteen-year-olds. He did it because he wanted to support anything that got the kids up and out the door at 6:00 a.m. He joked it was the only time he never had to badger them to get going. But I have thought a lot about surfing—the process of surfing—and how it is so apt for what we are talking about.

When facing a wave, you can fight it, be overwhelmed by it, or learn how to harness its power. When you think of society as a powerful wave—its constant motion and energy can either knock you down or propel you forward, depending on how you choose to interact with it. Instead of fighting against the current or getting swept away by the chaos, surfing allows you to ride the wave, using its momentum to move you in the direction you want to go. In the context of the three pillars of body, mind, and finance, this means recognizing the flow of societal pressures and demands but learning to navigate them in a way that aligns with your own values and goals. By cultivating resilience and adaptability—whether through maintaining physical health, mental clarity, or financial focus—you can use society's energy to fuel your progress, rather than drain you.

Surfing the wave of societal influence means staying balanced, grounded, and intentional, allowing you to thrive within the system without being consumed by it. It is so easy to get trapped into a reactionary mindset and focus on the immediate societal-deemed "outrage of the moment" and be swept away by it instead of focusing on who we are, and what we want to achieve.

The surfer learns first which wave to take. In fact, it starts with them deciding if these waves are worth surfing in the first place. But once the surfer is out, they are the personification of relaxed readiness as they wait for their "set"—catching a wave from a series that offers the best conditions for performance—before quickly transitioning into a flow state as they spring into action. It is a great analogy because a successful surfer right sizes the challenge, masters through iteration, employs perfect practice, stacks and automates habits, lies in wait in relaxed readiness, and then once a decision is made deploys with conviction where all their parts are working together in the flow state to achieve.

The best surfers understand that they are always students of the ocean, constantly learning and adapting. Each wave offers new challenges, and surfers must be willing to accept that they don't have all the answers. This mindset encourages a continuous process of self-reflection and course correction—adjusting their positioning, timing, and techniques based on the ever-changing conditions in the water. Surfers know that arrogance or overconfidence can lead to mistakes, so they approach the waves with a sense of patience and adaptability, always willing to adjust their approach.

Humility in surfing is not just about staying safe; it's about maintaining a learner's mindset—acknowledging that mastery is a moving target, and that respect for the ocean requires an openness to growth and a constant willingness to adjust course. This attitude of humility and ongoing learning doesn't just serve surfers in the water; it reflects a life philosophy, teaching the value of embracing challenges, learning from them, and staying grounded even as we strive to improve.

One historical figure who exemplified the philosophy of "surfing the wave" of society without being overwhelmed by it is Marcus Aurelius, the Roman emperor and Stoic philosopher. Despite the immense pressures of ruling an empire and dealing with constant war, political intrigue, and personal challenges, Marcus Aurelius practiced a form of detached engagement with the world. His Stoic beliefs emphasized that while we cannot control external events or societal forces, we can control our reactions to them, and that true strength lies in maintaining inner calm and clarity amidst chaos. Tom Brady, Jeff Bezos, George Washington, and Matthew McConaughey are just a few notable believers in Stoicism. All have been individually successful, but does individual success based on a set of principles translate into the betterment for us as a collective?

This is a profound and timeless question that delves into the intersection of personal development, responsibility, and the greater good. The idea of whether the strong should devote themselves to service, or focus primarily on their own individual growth, touches on deep philosophical and ethical considerations.

From one perspective, focusing on the individual—be it through self-mastery, achieving a healthy mind, body, and financial standing—creates a foundation from which you can contribute to others more effectively. The analogy often used is that of the oxygen mask on an airplane: You must secure your own mask first before helping others. By ensuring your own well-being and stability, you're better equipped to be of service to others in a meaningful and sustainable way. If you are not physically, mentally, and financially healthy, your ability to contribute to the collective—whether through leadership, charity, or positive influence—will be limited.

On the other hand, there is a deeply ingrained moral and societal notion that those who are "strong" or capable have a responsibility to use their resources, talents, and energy to uplift the collective. This mindset is rooted in concepts like altruism and social responsibility, which argue that the strength of the individual is most valuable when shared for the benefit of the larger community. Is a dynamic balance to be found?

Self-actualization and service are not mutually exclusive; they are interconnected. A strong, healthy individual who has mastered their own body, mind, and financial standing has an immense opportunity to help others from a place of genuine strength, not from a place of depletion or obligation. The true power of the strong lies in their ability to serve with integrity, offering their talents, knowledge, and resources in a way that lifts others, without diminishing their own well-being. It is through this balance of self-care and service to others that the individual not only achieves their greatest potential but also becomes a force for collective good.

The key is not choosing one over the other but understanding that true fulfillment comes from a life that harmonizes personal growth with the well-being of the collective. The strong who dedicate themselves to service in a way that is grounded in self-sufficiency and health will not only thrive but create ripple effects of positive change that elevate everyone around them.

The quote "Do not try to do good, but let it be the by-product of your actions" speaks to the idea that living according to a strong set of principles or a moral code can naturally lead to positive outcomes without the need to actively focus on doing "good" in a direct or calculated way. If you commit to living with integrity, applying yourself fully, and executing actions based on values such as honesty, diligence, and respect, goodness will naturally flow from your choices and behaviours.

The essence of this philosophy suggests that goodness is not something you have to chase or force—it emerges as a natural consequence of living a life aligned with your values and purpose. When you focus on the process, the principles, and the quality of your actions, you are, in essence, contributing to the greater good without having to consciously "try" to do so. Your focus is on the right actions, not on the specific outcomes, and by doing so, good things—whether for yourself or for others—will unfold as a result. So, yes—if you follow rules, execute based on a strong code of conduct, and apply yourself fully, good will take care of itself. The change we need in the world won't be coming from top-down government-led reforms. Just like our own body, economic, and financial well-being for all needs a bottom-up approach.

CHAPTER 21

FINAL WORD–THE BIOLOGY OF BEING

"We are not thinking machines that feel, rather we are feeling machines that think".

—Antonio Damasio

As we conclude, let's consider a powerful parallel between markets and human biology—both are complex energy systems that require balance and optimization. Today's market echoes the year 2000, when technology stocks commanded extreme valuations while critical resources were profoundly undervalued. Just as AI is today's transformative force, the internet was revolutionizing everything then. But beneath the surface, we're witnessing the same dangerous imbalance: Critical resources are becoming the biggest bottleneck for future growth. The world's transition to clean energy and digital infrastructure requires massive amounts of copper, nickel, lithium, uranium, molybdenum, rare earths, and other critical minerals—yet investment in new resource development has been woefully inadequate.

This sets up a powerful dynamic: The most over-owned stocks may deliver negative real returns for years, while resource sectors are poised for dramatic outperformance. When the world needs more of something that's increasingly difficult to produce, prices must rise. This principle of energy scarcity and value applies not just to markets, but to our own biological systems.

"Reason cannot defeat emotion, an emotion can only be displaced or overcome by a stronger emotion".

—Baruch Spinoza

The strategies presented here work because they work on a biological level. When we speak of energy management, we're not dealing with abstract concepts but with the very real, physical processes occurring within our cells. Consider every decision you make, every goal you set, every moment of inspiration or doubt—all of these experiences are rooted in biological processes. As Damasio's research shows, even our most rational decisions are guided by emotional markers, which themselves are biological signals.

When you're feeling alive, optimistic, and passionate, it's not just a psychological state—it's well-functioning systems biology, from your mitochondria to your neural networks. This is why our practices focus on optimizing your biological systems first. When your biology is functioning optimally, everything else follows—clearer thinking, better decisions, stronger motivation, and more sustainable energy.

The miracle of human achievement lies in our ability to harness these incredible biological systems. When humans operate at peak form, when our biology is optimized and our energy systems are aligned, we can accomplish what seems impossible. This is not metaphysical speculation—it's biological reality.

"What lies behind us and what lies before us are tiny matters compared to what lies within us".

—Ralph Waldo Emerson

I've always been captivated by the coastal Georgian Bay pines. Imagine a tiny seed crossing miles of rough waters, somehow finding its way into a crack in the weathered rock of a remote island. The odds of that seed not just surviving, but thriving, mirror our own unlikely existence.

These trees don't just survive—they tell stories through their twisted forms. When their original growth path is blocked, they don't give up; they branch out in new directions, often reaching greater heights than before. Throughout my life, I've veered off course more times than I can count, making both minor miscalculations and major missteps that could have easily derailed my journey entirely. Like these resilient pines I've always found a way forward.

When I see these trees, I'm reminded that our greatest stories aren't about avoiding obstacles, but about how we overcome them. They embody the spirit of transformation this book explores: the mindset of turning challenges into opportunities for growth, and the courage to branch out in new directions when our original path is blocked.

"The energy of the mind is the essence of life".

—ARISTOTLE

ACKNOWLEDGMENTS

I want to express my heartfelt gratitude to my family, friends, and coworkers—both past and present—who have supported me throughout my journey. Thank you for standing by me during my lowest moments, for celebrating my victories, and for helping me evolve. A special note of thanks to everyone who took the time to read and improve the many drafts of this book. I'm forever grateful.

EMBARK ON YOUR NEXT CHAPTER

But this book is just the beginning. Visit energeticmedia.com to dive deeper into these life-changing principles. Discover the C4 Model in action, gain exclusive investment and wellness strategies, and connect with a passionate community of like-minded individuals. Take the first step today and transform your life from the inside out!

www.ingramcontent.com/pod-product-compliance
Lightning Source LLC
Chambersburg PA
CBHW071202210326
41597CB00016B/1642